CW01379099

ONCE A DOCTOR, ALWAYS A DOCTOR

Heinz and Herta Hartmann. Breslau, Germany, 1938.

The Hartmann family (clockwise from left): Eleene Seeber, Michael, Joan, Mel, Heinz, Herta, Maurice, and Sarah.

Hartmann's seventieth birthday party: Heinz, center, was reunited with friends Erwin Zadik and Ken Walton, above, from his school days in Germany. Hartmann's wife, Herta, is on his left; on his right is his friend Congressman George Wortley.

ONCE A DOCTOR, ALWAYS A DOCTOR

THE MEMOIRS OF A GERMAN-JEWISH IMMIGRANT PHYSICIAN

Heinz Hartmann, M.D.

PROMETHEUS BOOKS
700 East Amherst St., Buffalo, New York 14215

ONCE A DOCTOR, ALWAYS A DOCTOR. Copyright © 1986 by Heinz Hartmann. All rights reserved. Printed in the United States of America. No part of this book may be used or reproduced in any manner whatsoever without written permission, except in the case of brief quotations embodied in critical articles and reviews. Inquiries should be addressed to Prometheus Books, 700 East Amherst Street, Buffalo, New York 14215.

Library of Congress Cataloging-in-Publication Data

Hartmann, Heinz, 1913-
   Once a doctor, always a doctor.

    Bibliography: p.
    1. Hartmann, Heinz, 1913- . 2. Jews, German—New York (State)—Syracuse—Biography. 3. Jews—New York (State)—Syracuse—Biography. 4. Physicians—New York (State)—Syracuse—Biography. 5. Syracuse (N.Y.)—Biography. I. Title.
F129.S8H23 1986   610'.92'4   86-42573
ISBN 0-87975-342-0

To all my loved ones: the deceased and the living.

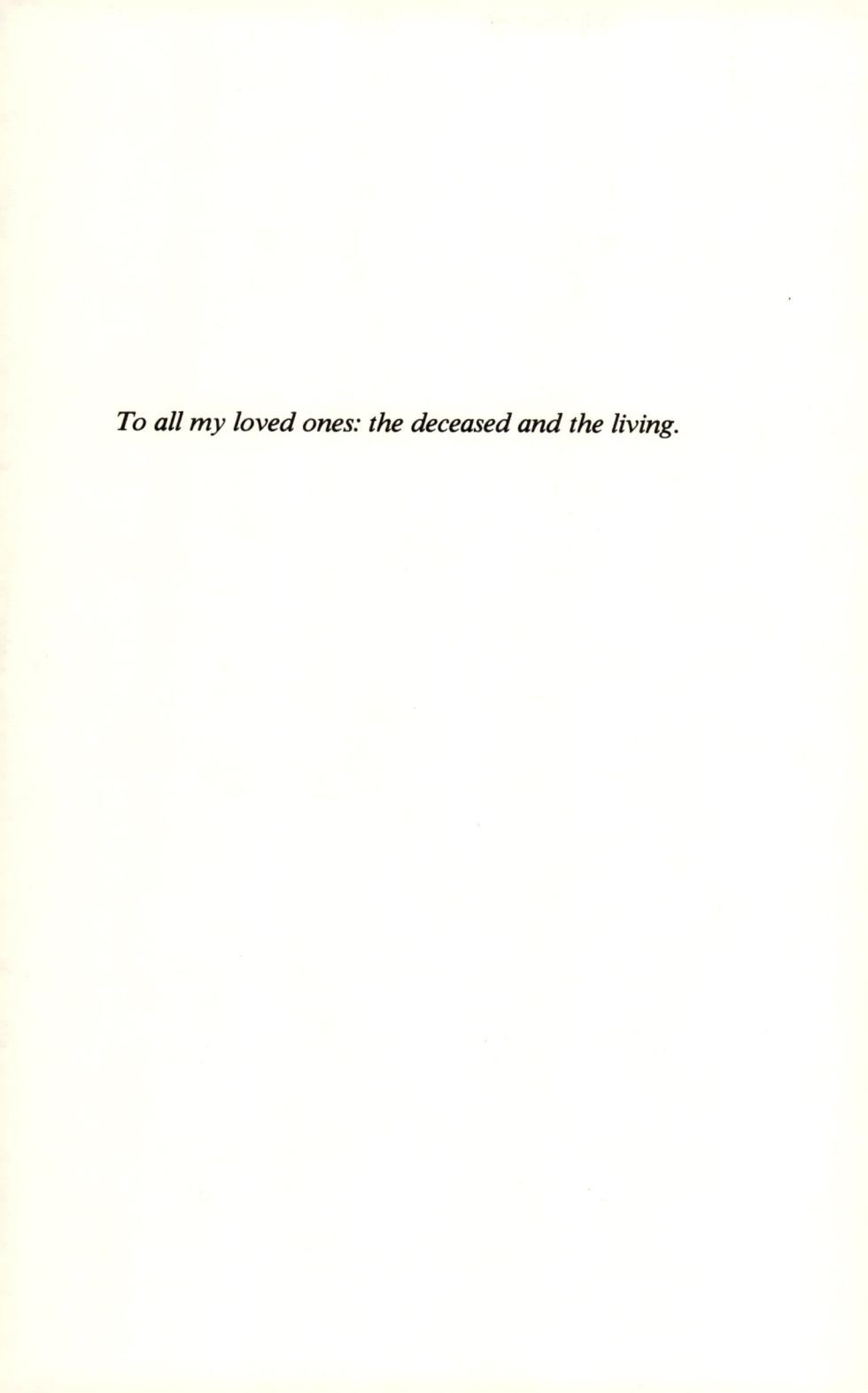

Table of Contents

Introduction	11
Breslau	13
Once a Doctor . . .	19
Once a Jew . . .	27
Emigration	31
Resettlement	35
Tully	41
New Life	47
Practice	51
"Missionaries"	55
Voyage of the Damned	59
California	63
Breakdown	65
. . . Always a Jew	71

Table of Contents

History of Jews in Syracuse	77
Michael	81
Atonement	89
In-Laws	95
Psychiatry	97
Heritage: Jews in Christian Heaven	103
Frustrations	113
Judaic Studies	119
Coincidences	127
Syracuse: City of Diversity	135
Second Career	139
Grandchildren	147
Seventieth Birthday Party	153
Retirement	159
Visits	167
On Writing	173
. . . Always a Doctor	179
Afterword	183
Recommended Reading	187

Introduction

It is hard to explain why I decided to write my autobiography. I don't have the political knowledge of our former presidents Nixon, Ford, and Carter, or of a Henry Kissinger, or a Theodore White; I certainly don't have the charm of a Lauren Bacall, a Shelley Winters, an Ingrid Bergman, a Gene Tierney, or a Lilli Palmer. And I surely don't have the brains of a Mortimer Adler, a Will Durant, or an Isaac Asimov. Writing all these famous names down, it comes to mind that the public might want to hear the story of just an "ordinary" person for a change.

I have to admit that since my immigration to the United States in 1939, I have not been back to Germany or to any other European country, and I have never been to Israel. Yet, as Carl Gustav Jung wrote of his life in *Memories, Dreams, Reflections,* all the outer aspects of my life, like travels and encounters with famous people, are just "accidental"; only my "inner experiences" count for my Life-Development.

Being a doctor is another justification for writing my story. There is always interest in and misconception about the medical profession. Who does not know about "Marcus Welby, M.D.," a physician in family practice who makes house-calls, has office hours, assists at surgery, and still finds the time to attend bar mitzvahs, weddings, and funerals? Television's "General Hospital," "The Practice," and "Trapper John, M.D." are watched by huge audiences.

Yet a much more serious reason for my writing these memoirs was expressed by Rabbi Nahman of Bratslav and in

Voices of Wisdom, by Francine Klagsbrun: "He who is able to write a book and does not write it, is as one who has lost a child."

Breslau

The small town where I was born in 1913 was Ostrow, Prussia; that place is Polish now. My fondest memory of Ostrow is a letter written by an older couple from San Francisco who had visited my parents during the Passover holidays. They had enjoyed our company during their stay and praised my parents for having such a nice baby (me). Along with their warm letter they sent us a silver spoon on which the Golden Gate Bridge was engraved. I treasured both letter and silver spoon for many years. In 1939, when my emigration to the United States could no longer be delayed, I sent that letter to my prospective sponsor in San Francisco; she happened to be the daughter of the old couple, and she was also my aunt. This sentimental letter, along with a visit from my friend Fred S. Preuss, helped to persuade Aunt Jenny Krotoczyner to issue an affidavit for both my wife and myself. Mrs. Krotoczyner was the widow of a physician, who—as the story went—defended the German people in World War I and was shot by a deranged patient in his office. The letter became the possession of my sponsor, and the silver spoon from San Francisco was lost several years later, after we had moved to Tully, New York. In any case, I shall always be grateful to this aunt of mine for making it possible for my wife and me to enter these United States.

As my parents, Moritz and Sarah Hartmann, and my older sister Kate were raised in German culture and were only able to converse in the German language, after World War I we moved to Breslau, Silesia, in eastern Germany, which is now the city of

Wroclaw in Poland. I must have been about seven years old when I arrived with my parents and Kate in Breslau, a city of about 600,000 people, approximately 11,000 of them Jews. Breslau had good schools, a well-known university, beautiful theaters, and a famous opera house. There is an old German proverb, "Every second Berliner is from Breslau." Scientists, artists, actors, opera singers, and medical teachers, after they had made their mark in Breslau, were called away to Berlin and many other metropolitan centers.

One famous native of Breslau was neurosurgeon Otfried Foerster. Wilder Penfield, a neurosurgeon who became one of the most illustrious physicians of our time, was very interested in the surgical treatment of epilepsy, in which Dr. Foerster excelled, so Penfield spent six months of postgraduate study under Foerster in Germany. It did not take Penfield very long to learn German as Fräulein Bergman, his children's governess, spoke no English at all. Soon, Penfield had the opportunity to watch Foerster operate in the Wenzelhanke-Krakenhaus operating room where another famous Breslau surgeon, Professor Kuetner, also worked. While in the Breslau suburb of Obernigk, Penfield was summoned by the police to treat an American boy suffering from epileptic seizures. Penfield was unable to treat the boy in Breslau as he was a private patient of Foerster, but years later, Dr. Penfield performed brain surgery on him in the United States. The boy's mother, Mrs. William Ottman, never forgot the good doctor, and, some years later, when the Montreal Neurological Institute, where Dr. Penfield did most of his research, was in financial trouble, the wealthy lady was ready with a large donation.

I met Penfield's son, A. Jefferson Penfield, many years ago at a party given by Dr. David Nash, a professor of medicine and the author of several medical books. The younger Penfield, a noted gynecologist and obstetrician, entertained everyone at the party by playing some German tunes on the piano. Apparently, they were melodies his father had learned in Breslau. What a small world!

Wilder Penfield finished his autobiography, *No Man Alone,* in 1976, three weeks before his death at the age of 85. This giant of medicine, who was even called to the Soviet Union for consultations during the cold war, also wrote fiction, including *The Torch,* a historical novel about Hippocrates.

Another great neurosurgeon, Dr. Ludwig Guttmann, also worked in Breslau, first as chief assistant to Professor Foerster and later as chairman of the Neurological Department at the Breslau Jewish Hospital. When I was one of the interns there, Guttmann read a letter to us that he had received from the famous Boston neurosurgeon Dr. Harvey Cushing. The letter was full of praise for one of Dr. Guttmann's books, so "typical of German ambitiousness." In 1939 this German-Jewish doctor succeeded in immigrating to England, where he soon was able to develop new methods of treating soldiers' spinal injuries. He was knighted by the Queen, and streets were named after this eminent physician, who—according to Nazi doctrine—belonged to an inferior race.

The University of Breslau counted world-famous names among its teachers. There were the physiologists Heidenhain and Purkinje, the pathologist Julius Cohnheim, and Albert Neisser, who discovered the gonococcus, the micro-organism causing gonorrhea. Ferdinand Cohn, the botanist, worked extensively in the field of bacteriology, preparing the way for Robert Koch, who discovered the tubercle bacillus. Professor Oscar Minkowski, the internist, published important papers about diabetes mellitus. They all, Jews and non-Jews, worked hand in hand until the great darkness befell Germany.

I attended the Koenig Wilhelms Gymnasium in Breslau, a so-called humanistic gymnasium where we were taught Latin and Greek and learned to read poets and philosophers in their native (now "dead") languages. Never did I regret this long and arduous humanistic education. Although it served no immediate practical purpose, its value in my later scientific and medical development cannot be overemphasized.

In the lower grades of the gymnasium there were a few Jewish students, but in the middle and upper grades I was the only Jewish boy in my class. All of the Jewish boys in the class pictures that I still possess were miraculously able to get out of Germany in the nick of time. I have been able to locate them, one by one, in the United States. The first I was able to contact was Felix Taucher; he died of a heart condition in Joplin, Missouri, about four years ago. Then I found Ken Walton, formerly Kurt Wartenberger, whose father was a cantor at Breslau's New Synagogue. Ken, whose son is a psychiatrist who studied at Syracuse Medical College, resides in Rochester, New York. Just a few months ago, I found Erwin Zadik in the Bronx; he had arrived in the United States many years ago after a temporary stay in Shanghai. I had not seen him for nearly sixty years.

I remained in constant touch with my friend Fred Preuss, who had been a grade ahead of me in school and was able to immigrate to this country before I did. He is now a pathologist in Texas. I was even able to locate a non-Jewish classmate of mine, Dr. Franz Josef Nave, who works as a pediatrician in Cincinnati. He came to this country after finishing his medical studies in Germany. His father had lost his job as a judge in Germany because he opposed the Nazi regime.

I found these classmates through the columns of *Aufbau,* a German-Jewish weekly paper published in New York City. Now in its fiftieth year, *Aufbau* was founded by Manfred George, a well-known Berlin journalist. Since George's passing, it has been published by the able Hans Steinitz.

In general, neither teachers nor students discriminated against me while I attended the higher grades of the Breslau gymnasium. But that was, of course, before the advent of the Hitler era. While the other pupils were receiving instruction in Catholic or Protestant religion, my rabbi, Dr. Goldschmidt, came to my classroom especially to give me the weekly one-hour instruction in Judaism. As I was his only charge at the time, he allowed me to choose the topics. I remember, among other things, wanting to hear about Baruch Spinoza's break with Judaism and excommunication from the Jewish community. Outside school, I learned the Hebrew Bible and even portions of the Talmud.

Breslau was the seat of the Jewish Theological Seminary, and it was from there that the three branches of Judaism originated. Born of Jewish parentage and growing up in Breslau, it was practically impossible to forget about my Jewish heritage. While in high school, I went with a Jewish youth group to the south of Germany and visited important cities including Nüremberg, which would become most infamous during the Third Reich. We also visited Prague, the capital of Czechoslovakia. Prague is the home of the Old New School, one of the oldest synagogues of Europe; of the legendary Rabbi Loew, the creator of the "golem"; and of Franz Werfel, Max Brod, and Franz Kafka.

In 1932, I took a trip to Vienna, the capital of Austria. There I met my cousin Ernst Schweiger, the son of a rabbi, who is now a physician in Portsmouth, Virginia. I also attended the Vienna Volksopera and the theater on the Josefsstadt.

People in Vienna asked me many questions about the turmoil at Breslau University: Ernst J. Cohn, a young Jewish law-scholar, had been appointed head of the law department at the University that year but was forced to resign. Student demonstrations and disturbances of all kinds had prevented him from giving his lectures. He emigrated soon after and became a well-known barrister and teacher of law in London.

Another of my experiences in Vienna sticks in my mind: I climbed the stairway to Siegmund Freud's office on Berggasse 19. I was fascinated by the man, and it gave me some satisfaction to see his place of work, even from the outside. It was quiet on the second floor of Berggasse 19, and I remember reading in various biographies that Freud's pupils and friends did everything possible to keep unwanted visitors or would-be patients away from their great teacher.

Whenever I traveled by train, I took a supply of Vasano, the anti-motion sickness medication, with me. Only in that way was I able to read the *Berliner Tageblatt* or the *Vossische Zeitung* during my long train rides.

In 1931 I finished my high school education. The National Socialist party was not in power, and anti-Semitism was not yet legal. As I was the only Jewish pupil in the upper grades of the gymnasium, I naturally became more and more intrigued by some people's attitude toward Jews, and I continued to search for my own identity. It was clear to me that there was more hatred for Jews in small communities, where there was little contact with them, than in large cities like Berlin, where people of diverse backgrounds worked together.

Every Jew, it seemed, was told by at least one non-Jewish friend: "If only every Jew were like you, there would be no anti-Semitism. . . ." At the same time, this story was making the rounds: Two acquaintances were talking, and the one, who was a bigot, said to his friend, "The Jews are to blame for everything." "Yes," the friend answered, "the Jews and the bicyclists." "Why the bicyclists?" the anti-Semite questioned. "Why the Jews?" the friend replied. Also well-known is the tale about Karl Lueger, former mayor of Vienna, who was famous for giving frequent anti-Semitic speeches. When he was asked how, in spite of this fact, he had so many Jewish friends, he replied, "I determine who is a Jew."

The time of my arbitur came in 1931. The arbitur is an oral examination feared by 18-year-old students because it was so difficult. As I remember, the subjects on which I was tested were Greek and religion. My dear father, who was a member of the B'nai B'rith Lodge, used to bring home Jewish books from the library, and this piqued an interest in my heritage that has never waned. Dr. Goldschmidt questioned me about Judaism, its culture, and its influence throughout history. My presentation must have made an impression on all my non-Jewish peers, since one of them reported to me that Dr. Jahn, the principal, was "quite overwhelmed and could not get over" many of the historical facts I managed to discuss. It was 1931, but the fact remains that the schools in Germany did not teach much about Jews, Judaism, or even the Old Testament.

Once a Doctor . . .

After graduating from high school, I enrolled at Breslau University to study medicine. There was never really any doubt in my mind that I wished to become a physician. (I knew full well that I was not fit for any of the business professions.) Since my early school years I wanted to become a doctor. Although our family, myself included, did not suffer from serious illness, what a difference it made to us when the family physician arrived to make us feel better! When the psychological writings of Siegmund Freud and Wilhelm Stekel appeared, my desire to study the healing arts and to help mankind in some small way intensified. I never wavered, and neither did my Jewish classmates who had the same goals as I did. Surely, there have been aggravations over the years, even in this country: government interference and impossible malpractice fees, to name two. Yet, medicine remains one of the finest professions, and for me there is no other. Once a doctor, always a doctor.

In Germany, anybody who wanted to be a doctor was admitted to medical school and able to graduate as a doctor of medicine if he or she passed all the examinations and proved that he or she was qualified. As a matter of fact, there were American students there in 1931 (some of them Jewish), who could not get into American medical schools because of the "numerous clausus" and the quota system.

For the first two and a half years we had to study preclinical subjects like anatomy, physiology, chemistry, physics, botany, and pathological anatomy. At the end of that period we were required to pass an examination, the "physicum." Then we entered the clinical field and took courses in internal medicine, surgery, forensic medicine, psychiatry, obstetrics, and gynecology. During vacations we were able to work as externs or "famulus" to acquire some medical skills at the hospital. The complete medical course took six years, followed by internship and residency.

It was 1933 and the beginning of the Nazi era when we few Jewish medical students realized that we had gradually become more and more estranged from the rest of the class. I was walking to one of the medical lectures with a co-ed when she remarked that, while she admired me for having so many acquaintances and friends in medical school, it was only fair, in her opinion, to restrict the influence of Jews in Germany in science, literature, and medicine. "Something just has to be done," she said. Also, little by little, students we would never have suspected of belonging to the Nazi party appeared in brown Nazi uniforms. At the beginning of one lecture, one of them announced to the student-filled auditorium: "The Jewish students will have to sit in the three back rows; that is the most we can allow them." Little by little, we few Jewish students stopped talking to non-Jewish medical students; we listened to the lectures and presentations and went home to study for the examinations.

Breslau had a well-known medical faculty. There were several Jewish professors on the teaching staff, some of them department heads. Soon after I had passed my physicum, I saw a note that Professor Hans Winterstein, chief of physiology, had written and pinned to his office door. The note said that he heard it was rumored that he had made disparaging remarks about Reichschancellor Adolf Hitler. This accusation was not true, the note said. Dr. Winterstein had been brought up in the Christian faith, but one Jewish grandparent was enough to discredit him. He was eventually invited to teach physiology at the University of Istanbul.

Pharmacology was taught by Professor Otto Riesser, a descendant of Gabriel Riesser—a nineteenth-century Jewish judge who fought for the emancipation of the German Jews. One day, when Professor Riesser attempted to start his lecture, students stomped their feet, howled, and jeered, and Riesser was forced to stop. He was brave enough, and he was unruffled as he told them that he had been fighting a war for Germany while they were still in diapers. It was to no avail; he was forced out.

I also remember Johannes Lange, professor of psychiatry, who during those turbulent years had divorced his Jewish wife and so was able to continue to teach. He entered the auditorium with the Hitler Salute, as expected, and, on, the chancellor's birthday he made a little speech, as expected. He did not say much except to admonish us to do the work, just "as our Fuehrer works for us all the time." Then he sat down—tired, it seems in retrospect. He died a short time later of endocarditis lenta, an inflammatory disease of the heart. A tragic end to a promising life.

Wilhelm Stepp, author of a book about vitamins, was the chief of internal medicine. Before he left the University of Breslau for a better offer at Münich, he reminded us that, years before the Nazi regime had come into power, he already had sympathized with them. He alluded to a well-known story about how he had flunked a Jewish student who later committed suicide. At the time of the incident, there was quite an uproar, as I remember, in the German press, which questioned whether the treatment of the Jewish student was justified. After the war, the American news media interviewed Professor Stepp who, according to the *A.M.A. Journal,* acted surprised when told about how badly the Jews were treated by the Nazis in the concentration camps. He said he didn't know that.

The last Jewish professor to leave the Breslau Medical faculty was Max Jessner, descendant of a famous theatrical family, who was the chairman of dermatology. Apparently it was hard to find an Aryan replacement for the Department of Skin Diseases, which had been previously headed by another Jew, Josef Jadassohn. Jessner was, in time, able to escape to Switzerland and later to the United States.

Although the worst of the Nazi evil had not yet befallen us, in recollecting my years of training for the medical state board, I remember vividly the story of James Meredith, the first black man to be enrolled at the University of Alabama. The governor himself physically blocked the entrance to the college. Mr. Meredith was given police protection to enter the classroom, and the press later asked him questions about his adjustment. His answer was an understatement I was never able to forget: "The atmosphere is not conducive to learning. . . ."

It was 1933 when Jews began to be arrested on the pretense of *Rassenschande,* an affair with a German, non-Jewish girl. Stores owned by Jews had been boycotted. Some Jewish physicians, including those who had fought for Germany in the First World War, were permitted to practice freely for a while, but it was not long before Jewish doctors were only able to take care of non-Aryan patients. Jews were not allowed to attend shows or concerts. It was then that a *Kulturbund* (organization for culture) was formed, consisting of great actors and actresses, conductors, and musical artists, who, because of their Jewish birth, had been forcibly removed from German culture. The president of Breslau's Jewish community at that time, Doctor of Law Ernst Rechnitz, wrote an article in the Jewish community paper comparing the German Jews to biblical Joseph, and the non-Jewish population to Joseph's brothers. When Joseph received the gift of a many-colored coat from his father, Joseph's brothers were jealous and sold him into slavery; when the Jews became successful, their neighbors became jealous and tried to destroy them. It was certainly brave of Dr. Rechnitz to write his honest opinion, but the Nazi authorities considered it *Greuel-Propaganda* (a horror story), and he was arrested. Luckily, he was later able to escape to South America.

In the mid-1930s, some Jews managed to go to Palestine. Others found it possible to leave for Shanghai, which had an open immigration policy at that time. England accepted men into an interim refugee camp and women as domestics, which they badly needed. But our small Jewish group at Breslau's Medical College was not ready to leave Germany yet. It was the dream of all of us to emigrate to the United States, but we had to take our state board first, to insure our future as physicians, and we were forced to wait until our quota was called by the American Consulate in Berlin.

Meanwhile, we were put into two small examination groups, along with a Christian girl who had the prefix "von" in front of her name, signifying that she had descended from German nobility. The authorities must have found a Jewish grandmother or grandfather in her family tree, and so she joined the Jewish students for her state board.

We passed our medical state boards, and I, like the rest of the medical students, had to serve an internship—the practical year. The only hospitals open to Jewish interns or residents were Jewish ones. I fulfilled my internship obligations at Breslau Jewish Hospital, while my friend Fred Preuss served his practical year at the hospital of Hamburg's Jewish community. The year ended, and in 1937 I was eligible to receive a medical license in Germany. What I actually got was a letter from the Ministry of the Interior stating I had satisfied all the requirements for my medical license but one—Aryan descent. I stayed on as an assistant resident at the Breslau Hospital, and wrote my doctoral dissertation about a "rare affliction with esophagus neurosis" on a case from the clinic of well-known Jewish internist Professor Harry Schaeffer. This paper was accepted by Professor Isenschmid from the University of Berne in Switzerland, where I had to matriculate for one semester to receive my diploma as a doctor of medicine.

People in neutral Switzerland were generally well-informed about the events in Germany. When I registered at Berne University, one of the women at the office shook my hand and said that eventually everything would turn out all right, that "we Catholics and you Jews have to stick together." There was, of course, no chance for any of us to stay in safe Switzerland. First, our loved ones were still in Germany. And, as soon as we arrived, we found notes at our hotel rooms telling us to report to the Foreign Police. They wanted to hear again and again when we had arrived, how long we were going to stay, and why we were there.

Of course, I do have pleasant memories of weekend excursions to neighboring resort areas. Interlaken and the bigger Montreux were towns where French was predominantly spoken. Berne was the capital, with a mainly German-speaking population, while in other areas Italian was spoken. I think it was in

Montreux that I desired two soft-boiled eggs for breakfast. There was a sign on the window of that restaurant: *Hier wird Deutsch gesprochen* (German spoken here). I entered the place, but it was hard for the management to find a qualified translator. Finally, they got hold of a young man who claimed to understand me, but they served me two *hard*-boiled eggs.

Aside from writing a doctoral dissertation, medical students had to take an oral examination in two medical subjects. I was examined in forensic medicine by Professor Dettling and in surgery by the world-famous Professor de Quervain. Not that those were my favorite subjects—I would rather have selected internal medicine or a similar topic, but I was advised that some of the professors were Nazi sympathizers. Even here, in neutral Switzerland, one had to be selective in choosing one's examiner. At last I received my medical diploma from the University of Berne in February 1938.

I returned to Germany, where I resumed my work as an assistant resident at the Breslau Jewish Hospital. Getting out of Germany was foremost on the minds of young Jewish doctors like me. While waiting for our quotas, we studied the English language. I remember reading Sinclair Lewis's *Arrowsmith* and studying Rypins' *Medical State Board Examinations* in preparation for my hoped-for future medical career in the United States.

In October 1938, I married Herta Friedman. We had met at the Breslau Jewish Hospital where Herta was a nurse and had worked with me on the medical, surgical, and neurological wards. I was, in her opinion, "sincere, smart, a good human being, and a good doctor." We were working closely together, we had the same goals, and we fell in love. After her graduation as a registered nurse in 1935, we decided to get married. First, however, I had to finish my medical education in Switzerland, so, I would meet Herta at my parents' home and at the home of her mother. I also visited her at the Home for Nurses, where she lived. The threat of Nazism was already serious, and there were restrictions for Jews about going out at night, so we were not permitted to attend theater performances or movies in the evening.

Still, Jews waiting for their exit visas were not idle; cultural activities abounded in early- and mid-1938. The *Kulterbund* performed Lessing's *Nathan, the Wise* before Jewish audiences, while orchestras composed of Jewish musicians and led by world-famous Jewish conductors performed works of Mozart, Mendelssohn, and Brahms. Jewish scholars like the philosopher-theologian Martin Buber and Alfred Adler, founder of Individual Psychology, discussed their work in crowded lecture halls.

But, in November of that year, trouble began in earnest. A young Polish Jew, Herschel Gryneszpan, shot and killed Ernst von Rath, the secretary of the German Embassy in Paris, after hearing about the persecution of his parents whom he had left behind in Nazi Germany. That same month, the "Crystal Night" took place.

Once a Jew . . .

On the night of November 9, 1938, Jewish stores were vandalized and plundered, synagogues were burnt down, and shattered glass from broken windows, lamps, and displays covered the streets. This was Crystal Night. That night, the non-Aryan men were rounded up and taken to concentration camps. Two weeks after my wedding, I was taken with so many, many others, including Herta's brothers Herbert and Erwin, to Buchenwald Camp. We did not know of any "crime" we had committed except for the fact that we had been born Jewish. Herta and other nurses stood in front of the hospital, watched, and cried.

When our unhappy crowd of prisoners was assembled in one of the large Breslau courtyards, an elderly police officer tried to console us, intimating that our incarceration would be a short one and everything would eventually be all right for us. He certainly sympathized with us, but he had no insight into what was going on. When we finally arrived at Weimar, near our destination, some of the spectators were shaking their heads sadly. They must have seen similar transports before.

We were all thrown together at Buchenwald: doctors, lawyers, laborers, teachers, rabbis, even priests and ministers who had a Jewish grandparent. We had to report for a roll call every day. We stood in line for our watery soup. On the advice of older inmates, we tried to suck on buttons we had saved to quench our thirst. We "slept" in crowded, wooden barracks for a few hours during the night. Of course, there were beatings and even shootings of prisoners, but this concentration camp was nothing compared to the extermination camps like Auschwitz, Birkenau, and Treblinka in the later years of Nazism.

After six or eight weeks we saw the release of the first "November action" prisoners. We were even permitted to send a postcard to our loved ones at home, but we were told what to write: "I am sitting here, and I feel quite well. . . ." Finally, at the time of our discharge, we had to sign a statement testifying to how nicely we had been treated. Luckily, nobody refused to sign.

In the meantime, Herta, with the other nurses and the few remaining physicians, had been working day and night at the Jewish Hospital treating Jews who'd attempted suicide, those who'd had nervous breakdowns, and others who'd been released from the concentration camps with typhoid, malnutrition, and physical and mental wounds. Herta had heard about Jewish persons who had died at Buchenwald and whose ashes had been returned to their families, and she was worried about me. Wearing her nurse's uniform, she went to Gestapo Headquarters, but they would not give her any kind of information about me. She was relieved when she finally received my postcard telling her that I was still "alive."

Finally, in late December 1938, I was released and arrived at Breslau's main railroad station, Hauptbahnhof. I had a chance to be reunited with my parents, Herta, and my older sister Kate. She had been divorced one or two years before but had sent her boy Joachim to be with her former husband, who had been able to escape to Palestine. Also discharged with me from Buchenwald were my wife's brothers, Herbert and Erwin. I went back as an assistant resident to the Hospital of the Jewish Community, which had been taken over by some designated members of the Nazi party, non-Jewish nurses, and domestics. The Jewish doctors could still prescribe medication for their patients, but they had to be extremely careful not to act in any way that could be interpreted as hostile to the Third Reich.

This "mild" concentration camp incarceration had shown us how urgent it was for us Jews to leave Germany as quickly as possible. It was clear that the Nazis intended to get rid of us, which was only right from their diabolical point of view. After all, the Jews had given the Bible to the world, and even the most estranged one remembers the old sayings: "Love your neighbor as yourself," "You shall not insult the deaf or put a stumbling block before the blind," "Do not judge your fellow man until you have stood in his place," "A person who publicly shames his neighbor is like someone who has shed blood." All these Jewish rules did not fit into the Nazi dictionary. So, we had to report to the Gestapo once a month to report our "progress." We had, of course, applied for our American visas, but would there be time to wait for our quota? I would have been able to go to an interim camp for men in England, but I did not want to go alone. Herta was invited to work as a nurse in the Philippines, but she did not want to go alone. We heard there was a chance we could both get a Bolivian visa, but this rumor proved to be false.

Finally, in the autumn of 1939, we were invited to appear before the U.S. Consul in Berlin, and we received our long-awaited American visas.

Emigration

It was not easy for Herta and me to leave my parents and older sister and her mother and younger brother behind, but we had to leave. Remaining in Nazi Germany would have been suicidal, and our staying could not save the lives of our loved ones. We booked passage on a German boat, the *Bremen,* but Hitler had marched into Poland and did not want his boats exposed to dangerous mines, so the trip was cancelled.

At last we were able to book passage on the Swedish steamer *Drottningholm* in mid-October of 1939. Paying for the trip presented its own difficulties. The money for the tickets had to be deposited in American dollars at the office of the Swedish American Line in the United States. Luckily, Herta's brother, Herbert Friedman, who had started a furniture business on the U.S. West Coast, was able to pay half of our fare, while the other half was contributed by my good friend Fred Preuss, who had only been in the United States a very short time and was a medical intern. "Heinz can be so proud to have such friends," my brother-in-law remarked. And proud I was.

We were not permitted to bring much out of the country with us. We did not own any furniture, but Herta and I were able to bring along some clothes and part of our library. The books had to be inspected by a member of the Wehrmacht (German military machine), to the best of my recollection. I cannot tell what his qualifications were. I had packed some Hebrew books and some medical volumes, but I was careful to avoid contemporary Jewish writers like Friedrich Gundolf, whose big treatise about Goethe I left behind. I did not bring any books by the German-Jewish poet Heinrich Heine, who was not in good standing at the time. He had written, of course, the famous song *"Ich weiss nicht, was soll es bedeuten, dass ich so traurig bin"* (I don't know what it means, that I am so sad), but the public was informed that this wellknown poem was an old, old folksong. I did not dare take any books written by modern Jewish writers like Jakob Wassermann, Arnold and Stefan Zweig, Max Brod, Alfred Doeblin, and Franz Werfel. We were permitted to carry only about four dollars in cash per person, if memory serves me right; yet, we were not interested in books or money—we only wanted to get out of Nazi Germany.

A big "J" for *Jude* or Jew was stamped onto our passports. Every Jewish man was obliged to carry "Israel" as his middle name, and every Jewish woman had to use the name "Sarah." We were proud of both our original and our additional names. When in 1948 a Jewish state was formed, it was called Israel; my mother's name was Sarah, which also is the first name of my granddaughter.

With our new names and stamped passports, we set out by train on our journey to Sweden. After the long blackout in Nazi Germany, we were overcome with joy when we saw the first lights in Malmö. We knew then that we had crossed the border and were free.

We had heard that the waters of the ocean were mined, but this seemed a small risk—much smaller than living in Nazi Germany. We continued on to Göteborg, from where the *Drottningholm* was going to sail, where we were greeted by a Jewish reception committee. Herta and I stayed there two days, until the ship departed for the United States. We received an extra bonus at our hotel that first night: We had escaped war-torn Germany with its starvation-rationing for Jews, and we were hungry. Herta was craving some whipped cream. We didn't know one word of Swedish and so were unable to explain our wishes to the kitchen personnel, but they permitted us to look around in the kitchen, where we found plenty of whipped cream. They did not care that we ate so much; it did not make us sick either.

On the ship we were visited by a Director Huettner, an influential member of a well-known Swedish-Jewish family, who offered us refugees from Hitler's Germany a small "loan," which I (and others like me) accepted, after some hesitation. Although it was a small amount, I finally realized that the fine gentleman really did not expect anyone to pay it back. That was a tremendous relief, because I was not sure of our future, and I had to reimburse my in-laws and my friend for our boat tickets first. We had also to think of the dear family we had left behind and were hoping to be able to get out of their bondage as soon as possible.

Our first wedding anniversary was celebrated on the *Drottningholm*. One of our well-wishers was the steward of the ship, a man who never shied away from alcoholic drinks. He had been very happily married for twenty years, he said, and he wished us the same happiness. (Considering his occupation, though, I don't believe he was home with his wife too much.)

One night after we had retired, everything on the ship began to shake; furniture and luggage tumbled down. They called it Orkan 11, one of the biggest hurricanes ever. We two were the sickest on the boat and had to receive belladonna injections on two consecutive days. Finally, after two long weeks at sea, we were close enough to New York's harbor to be able to see the Statue of Liberty from afar. When we saw the Statue we felt that we had reached our main goal—to be free at last and not have to live any more in constant fear of being killed. We were saved a second time: First, we were able to get our visas to get out of Nazi Germany and to enter the United States, and now we had almost reached the United States of America. The ocean mines, the terrible storm, the seasickness—all this faded in our memories now. We were thankful to be alive and to be able to have a new beginning. Needless to say, we thought of the loved ones we'd had to leave behind in Nazi Germany. We had the best intentions, though, of getting our close relations out of that country any way possible.

Aside from us Jewish refugees, there were some German-

Americans on the boat who had visited relatives in their homeland and wanted to get back to the States since war had broken out. One of that group, a middle-aged gentleman who really took a liking to us, wished us well, but he warned us, as Jews, not to get involved with politics after our immigration. It seems that Henry Kissinger never received similar advice.

I was greeted at the pier in New York by my cousin Josef Hartmann and by Ruth, the wife of my cousin Ernst Hartmann. Josef had been the director of a candy company in Breslau, but now he worked in the assembly line in a baked-goods factory. On the day of our arrival, he took us to Horn and Hardert, a cafeteria "where the poor people eat," he explained. Ernst and Ruth invited us some Sundays later to our first movie at Radio City Music Hall. The feature was *Mr. Smith Goes to Washington,* starring Jimmy Stewart.

At first, the Jewish Refugee-Resettlement Committee gave us a room at the Congress House close to the Free Synagogue, where we attended our first Friday-night service. Rabbi Stephen S. Wise was the rabbi of that congregation, an imposing, tall gentleman, a friend of President Franklin Delano Roosevelt, and an internationally-known orator. I met him on the street later that year and had the courage to ask him for an affidavit for my parents and older sister whom I had left behind. He was friendly enough and advised me to contact his wife, Louise, who was specializing in and completely familiar with this matter. I did not follow Rabbi Wise's advice. Instead, I wrote to then New York State Governor Herbert H. Lehman and asked for an affidavit for my parents and sister, but I just received a form letter explaining that I would have to find private sponsors and go through the regular channels. That meant we had to go through all the red tape of getting affidavits and American visas for our relatives. It was all in vain; my parents and older sister never got out of Nazi Germany. On the West Coast, meanwhile, Herta's brother and sister-in-law tried their best to get their mother and younger brother admitted to the United States. They did not succeed either.

Resettlement

We were supported by the Refugee Committee for the Resettlement of Physicians. We rented a furnished room with kitchen-privileges in New York's upper Manhattan in Washington Heights, sometimes called "The Fourth Reich." I was able to purchase a small Emerson radio, which, combined with reading newspapers, helped me to prepare for the upcoming language examination. After I was notified that I had passed this barrier to practicing medicine in America, my next goal was to pass New York State's medical licensing examination. The Committee was good enough to sponsor some refresher courses for us. We younger physicians did not have it as hard as our older colleagues who had been out of medical school for so many, many years and had gotten rusty in theoretical subjects like anatomy, chemistry, and physiology, which they had not used in their actual medical practices in Germany.

In 1940, while waiting for the results of my medical state board examination, I took a job as an ambulance surgeon at New York's Knickerbocker Hospital where my friend Dr. Herbert Neisser was already working. It was a good experience for us as we were called to the homes of black, white, Irish, Hispanic, German, Polish, and native-born American people. When we were unable to treat patients on the spot, our ambulance took them to Knickerbocker, Harlem, Roosevelt, or, in psychiatric cases, Bellevue Hospital. We did not receive a salary, and we were on duty for twenty-four hours at a time. We would work from 7 A.M. one day to 7 A.M. the next; then we were supposed to have the next twenty-four hours off. It could happen, though, that a call would come in about five minutes before 7, and the poor doctor would end up being on for some additional three or four hours, losing out on his much-needed sleep. Just around that time I read in *Reader's Digest* a story about a young ambulance surgeon who was ready to go home from his twenty-four-hour service when one of these last-minute calls arrived. The driver took him to a far-away section of town. The young doctor went up a few flights of stairs, opened the door, and saw a young mother feeding her healthy-looking baby. "You know," she exclaimed, "I told you I would call the doctor if you didn't eat your cereal. . . ."

While waiting for the result of my medical licensure examination, I accepted an internship at the Nathan Littauer Hospital in Gloversville, New York. Herta, meanwhile, worked in New York City, about two-hundred miles away, as a special-duty nurse and in one of the private hospitals in Manhattan. Every four weeks or so, I would take a Sunday morning bus to Amsterdam, New York, and go by excursion train to New York City to meet Herta. In the afternoon I would make the return trip, arriving at Gloversville at about midnight.

While in Gloversville, I received my New York State medical license and was anxious to start my own practice. In order to do that, I first needed my driver's license—to find a place to practice we would have to drive through New York State. Even though I was 28 years old, I had never driven a car. Like most people in Germany, my main source of transportation had been my bicycle. A young man I met at the Jewish Community Center at Gloversville gave me my first driving lesson. I learned in my "new" secondhand 1933 Chevrolet and took and failed my first test in Fonda, New York.

I went to New York City to discuss the opening of my practice with the Resettlement Committee in Manhattan. They were willing to support us until we were able to stand on our own feet, but, in retrospect, it would have been more helpful if the committee had given us advice on where to settle, as information was more available to them than to us newcomers.

I registered with a driver education school and felt very well prepared when I took my first test in the big city. There was a rumor making the rounds at the time that you had to put a five dollar bill under the inspector's seat in order to pass; when another administration came, the story went, you failed if you tried this kind of bribery. I was never tempted to try that little trick, but after my examination the inspector told me, "That is all for today. . . ." This meant to me, fast thinker that I am, that I would have to come back. My conclusion was right, but I never did find out if I failed simply because I didn't leave a bribe. On one of the later tests the government official informed me, "I will see what I can do for you," and I received my driver's license in the mail.

Driving around in our old 1933 Chevrolet, we looked for a town where a physician was needed. In December 1941 we settled in Canajoharie, New York, not too far from Gloversville where I'd had my previous hospital job.

Canajoharie was a beautiful little town, seat of the Beechnut Company. We had some difficulties settling in, though. There was not much space available; I had to rent an upstairs apartment and use it for a small office and living quarters. Also, even with the war in full swing, people in this little community were very ill-informed about the Jews' place in history. "Aren't all the Jews originally from Poland?" a lady dentist asked me. And a gentleman remarked to me that it was brave indeed for a German to start the practice of medicine at that time in the United States of America.

As I knew that new physicians regularly got a write-up in the local newspaper when starting to practice in his chosen community, I went to the office of the Canajoharie weekly paper. The editor there assured me that she was not supposed to print anything like this. The other doctors wouldn't like it, she said, it was considered "unethical." After thanking her, I paid a friendly visit to some of Canajoharie's physicians and told about my experience with the newspaper. A short time later I found my story on its front page. It seems that Dr. Caroline Garlock had quizzed the editor about her refusal of my request. According to the physician, the following conversation took place:

"I don't want to print anything, because they are Nazis."
"How can they be Nazis? They are Jews who had to leave Nazi Germany."
"Well, then they are Jews, and I don't like Jews either."
"You print it," Dr. Garlock retorted, "and you print it on the first page!"

And she did. As a matter of fact, on Dr. Garlock's advice, Herta and I went to a church dinner to get better acquainted with the community and its people. The lady editor sat across from me and poured me some coffee. She was very friendly.

Patients saw me at the office, but my practice also included many home visits, and I used Amsterdam City Hospital and St. Mary's Hospital for cases requiring inpatient treatment. I remember vividly one confinement case. The rugged-looking husband contacted me months before his wife's baby was due and requested a home delivery. He assured me that money was being saved up to pay me. At their simple home the husband played the guitar in between his wife's labor pains, I stayed up all night, and finally the baby arrived. When I was ready to leave and asked the young man for my fee, he explained that his wife had told him all along that she was saving money; he assumed it was for the delivery, but now he discovered that she had saved it for something else. It was general practice all right.

Since my student days in Germany I had been interested in the treatment of psychological and emotional diseases. Before settling down in practice, I had discussed with Herta the possibility of specializing in nervous and mental diseases. She did not see eye to eye with me. In the United States, her argument went, with all its freedom of expression and freedom from want, there would be is no need for the treatment of psychiatric disease. Little did we know that all the freedom in the world is no guarantee of protection from emotional disorder.

My interest in psychoneurosis and psychosomatic disorders started during my student days in Breslau. In the Medical College library I got hold of Freud's books and some of Wilhelm Stekel's volumes. What made Stekel's books, like *Conditions of Nervous Anxiety and Their Treatment* and *Technique of Analytical Psychotherapy,* most important was Stekel's ability to communicate with the reader through thousands of impressive case histories. Even Freud, who had his differences with Stekel almost from the start, admired his intuition and depth.

Dr. Samuel Lowy wrote the introduction to at least one of Stekel's books. In 1964 I attended a meeting of the American Association of Psychosomatic Medicine at which Dr. Lowy was one of the speakers. He was leaving the New York hotel and about to enter the elevator when I asked him if he were the same Dr. Lowy who had written the introduction to Stekel's books. He seemed quite surprised that I, coming from a small place like Syracuse, where I was then practicing, would be familiar with his scientific history. He promised to send me a copy of his newest book *Should You be Psychoanalyzed?* He inscribed it: "For Dr. Heinz Hartmann, in appreciation of his interest in Psychodynamics."

Tully

In the autumn of 1942, I was asked by the Procurement and Assignment Service to serve the community of Tully, New York. Their physician, Dr. Marcus S. Richards, had left to serve in the Army. At that time, we immigrant physicians, who were not eligible as yet to receive a military commission, were often called into communities where doctors were urgently needed. And needed I was. The farming village of Tully had a population of about eight hundred, and many professional people from nearby Syracuse or Cortland had their homes in Tully or had camps at Tully Lake. My practice consisted mainly of office hours for routine and emergency care and numerous home visits by day and by night.

Once, when the pressure became a bit too much, I took the telephone receiver off the hook for a little while. I was startled when the sheriff showed up at my house. It seems that patients had called him to complain that my phone was "out of order."

The large number of patients wasn't all I had to adjust to. I was used to big cities with large streets and house numbers, and it was difficult for me to find my way through the farm town on house calls. To get to a patient's house, I'd have to "turn left at a red barn, pass a mailbox, go on three or four miles until a fork in the road . . ." and on and on. I was once on the phone with a new patient who tried to give me instructions on how to get to her house, and I heard on the other line the voice of the woman who had referred her to me. "He is awfully hard on directions," she said, "but otherwise you will have no trouble."

I was in great demand. Aside from home visits and office practice, I served as health officer and school physician for the community of Tully. Once after a winter home call in the country, I had a cough, chills, and a high fever, and on the advice of Herta and her obstetrician, Dr. Henry Hillel, I went to bed with bronchitis. Still, I dispensed medications for some of my ill patients. Dr. Hans Hirsch, another immigrant physician, came from nearby Cortland to examine me and give his medical advice. While in Tully, he even made two house calls for me.

Cortland is not too far from Tully, and I made contact there on weekends with some other refugee physicians. In Homer, a small town near Cortland, Herta and I became friends with Dr. Eugene Alexander from Berlin. His son Steven is now a family practitioner in Syracuse. One of my closest friends at that time was Dr. Hans Seligman, another immigrant physician. We became friends in Tully and visited each other until his untimely death, fourteen years later, at age 46. Dr. Seligman was crippled with rheumatoid arthritis and had ulcers, but he continued his family practice to the last. He was a very devoted physician, his goals were the same as mine, and we were about the same age. We spent many happy hours discussing medicine, practice, and family. My daughter Joan and his children Rudi and Esther grew up together. Hans took a special interest in my son Michael and other handicapped persons, and he always had new suggestions for treatment. His widow, Rita Seligman, has remained our friend through all the years since his passing.

We were the only Jewish people in Tully at the time, except for a lady gym teacher who worked in the Tully school system a while and for two or three farmers in the neighboring county. On the Jewish high holidays we had to attend services at one of Syracuse's synagogues. We became friends with the Reverend Cox, a Protestant minister, and his family, and with Catholic Father Ploeckl, of German descent, who served Tully's St. Leo Church. Ploeckl came to my aid more than once when I got stuck in my snow-covered driveway, and he got me out in no time at all. But, it was also more than once that we discussed with Father Ploeckl our worries about our loved ones who had remained in Nazi Germany, and we spoke about the evil deeds of that regime. *"Das kann ja nicht mehr lange dauern"* (It cannot last long anymore), he told us, because "they don't have the truth." Yet, it did last long, too long. His words reminded me of Dr. Hans Freund, an Orthodox Jew and a saintly man who was the last chief physician of Breslau Jewish Hospital's medical department. Whenever one of our interns or residents was able to emigrate, he always said, "Now you are going to leave, when all this will be over soon anyway?" He, unfortunately, never got out.

In January 1943 Herta, under the care of obstetrician Dr. Hillel, gave birth to Joan Suzanne. Joan was tiny, and there were a few medical problems after birth, but Dr. Robert C. Schwartz, a well-known pediatrician and founder of the Syracuse Cystic Fibrosis Clinic, solved all her medical difficulties for us.

Apparently, it was hard to find household help locally at that time, so we were lucky to get the services of our friend Eva Hadda, daughter of Breslau Jewish Hospital's surgical department chief, Dr. Siegmund Hadda. She had just arrived in the States and had worked temporarily in one of New York's tailor shops. She was a great help to us before Herta's delivery and for many weeks afterward.

Roads were often treacherous in the Tully area on winter home visits. One night I received a call for help from a family living on a hill, and Herta insisted on going along with me. As nobody else lived with us at the time, we had to leave the baby alone at home. While we were gone, we vividly imagined all the terrible things that could happen to an infant left alone. Luckily, Joan was sleeping peacefully in her bed when we returned, but we never forgave ourselves for that.

Practice in Tully gave me satisfaction, and I have many memories of those years. I was needed there. My prescriptions were filled at Wortley's Pharmacy. After Mr. Wortley Sr.'s passing, his son Edward took over the pharmacy, while his other son George became a member of the United States Congress.

Some medical cases stand out in my mind: A young lady who had lost a large amount of blood consulted me, and, after an examination and taking of her history, I diagnosed an ectopic, or tubal, pregnancy. I sent the patient to what was then the Syracuse General Hospital and received a kind and appreciative note from Dr. Lester Mellor, her obstetrical surgeon. The patient sent me a thankful letter expressing her pleasure and praising me at a time when doctors were easily criticized. I was young, and I felt flattered.

There was another case I will never forget—it is not too often that a man of 70 suffers from scarlet fever. On the advice of the patient's very nice family, I asked Dr. J. G. Hiss, one of the oldest living cardiologists, to come from Syracuse to Tully for a consultation. He is still, at the age of 90, medical officer for ACCORD, a senior citizens organization. At first he doubted my diagnosis, but when the patient started to peel, he concurred. Dr. Hiss took an EKG tracing at the bedside and gave advice, and the patient recovered.

Once I was called to the Tully home of a gentleman who must have been older than 80. His anxious family contacted me when the man had collapsed in front of the house and showed no signs of life. I was unable to detect a pulse or heartbeat, and there was obviously not much time to go into the man's medical history. I took a syringe and a vial of adrenalin from my bag and injected the medication into his heart. The man rose up from the ground slowly, opened his eyes, and asked a nearby relative, "What did you call the doctor for?"

Once, when a young farmer came down with a high fever but was otherwise not feeling too badly, I made a house call. Right away it seemed to me that he had undulant fever, or brucellosis, a disease caused mainly by the ingestion of raw, unpasteurized milk. I started the patient on the appropriate treatment, a sulfa preparation, and drew some blood for an agglutination test. Meanwhile, the young farmer's father asked me to call a consultant. One he suggested was Dr. Irving Ershler, a well-known Syracuse internist. "He is a landsman of yours," the patient's father told me. Knowing that the doctor had been born in America, I was puzzled by this statement. I found out later that he also was of the Jewish persuasion.

    Dr. Ershler and his wife, a registered nurse, came to Tully, and together we went to the farm. Dr. Ershler examined the patient and was sure that the fever was caused, not by brucellosis, but by an influenza virus. This fine doctor later founded the Syracuse Community General Hospital and served for a time as president of the Onondaga County Medical Society, but when we received the results of the agglutination test a few days later, it was strongly positive for brucellosis. Dr. Ershler phoned me from Syracuse and most graciously congratulated me, saying, "You know, one cannot always be right." Memories like this encourage me at times when my spirit gets a little low.

While we lived in Tully, Herta and I would often take summer vacations in the northern Catskill Mountains of New York. Fleischmanns, Margaretville, and some of the other resort towns there offered restaurants and entertainment European style, and it was possible to meet old acquaintances and friends there whom one never expected to find again in the United States. We also spent some time at Lake Placid and vacation spots in the Adirondack Mountains. In other years we went on vacation to Asbury Park or Atlantic City, where the big American Medical Association meetings were held every four years or so.

    I remember vividly one drive to the ocean resort. We were passing through the town of Nedrow when we saw a group of state troopers stopping every car. To my dismay, I suddenly realized that I had left my driver's license in my other suit at home. I realized, of course, that the troopers were probably out to find some criminal, perhaps even a murderer, but I turned around and headed home to pick up my hard-earned document. A state trooper saw me leaving, followed me, and made me stop. After I explained my intentions to the man in uniform, he reproached me saying, "Never do that, Doc, or you could get shot."

Naturally, I was not very pleased, but we were permitted to continue on our trip with the understanding that I would present my valid driver's license at the local police station after our return.

New Life

By 1945, Dr. Marcus Richards had returned to Tully from his service in the Army. He wanted me to stay in Tully, but I was ready to move on. Syracuse was twenty miles away; I had to visit patients at the hospital and attend lectures there, and the severe winters often made our return to Tully from the city very difficult. So, we decided to go to Syracuse.

We were in the process of moving when we received wonderful news from my in-laws in California: Herta's older sister, Lucy van der Linde, had been liberated and was coming with her five children to the United States. How she, a single Jewish woman (she'd been separated from Gerry, her half-Jewish husband, during the war), was able to survive and keep her children and herself hidden in the face of mortal danger is still not clear to me. It is almost unbelievable that they escaped the most dangerous situations, hunted and hungry and always afraid of being found out. After the liberation, Lucy's husband searched for her and their children. He found them in a liberation camp, and the whole family was able to emigrate together.

The go-between through whom we communicated with Lucy was a young psychiatrist, Lieutenant Max L. Wool. He went out of his way to visit liberation camps and bring gifts and comfort to all the inmates and so to Lucy. I had the good fortune to visit him and his dear wife and lovely family in Newton, Massachusetts. I was shocked and saddened to learn of this young, gentle man's fatal heart attack soon after.

It has been nearly forty years since Lucy's liberation. She is convinced that her miraculous escape from Nazi Germany was due to a guardian angel watching over her. Despite all the hardships she endured, she is not bitter toward anybody and never has anything bad to say about people.

About a dozen years ago, Lucy was the surprise guest on the Los Angeles television show "The Girl in Your Life." Everything had been secretly arranged by Hans, Peter, Ruth, Mary Ann, and Renee, her adoring children. The show's host had her tell about her experiences in Nazi Germany. And, as her gift for being on the show, she received a new piano—she had been a pianist for the silent movies when living overseas.

Whenever Lucy visits us from California, she is impressed by our doctor friends, who give her the royal treatment. According to Lucy, the physicians out West don't show her the same personal interest as do the doctors here. It was quite an experience when Lucy came to see us after she'd had a cataract operation on one of her eyes. Unfortunately, she told us, the surgery had not been a success. We subsequently found out that the glass over her operated eye was only window glass. We sent her to see Dr. Stanley Charlamb here, who prescribed the proper contact lens, and her problem was solved.

Lucy frequently volunteers her services at the Jewish Old Age Home or at the Ida Benderson Center for senior citizens when she visits us in Syracuse. At age 82 she is, fortunately for her, in much better health than the "younger" people she entertains.

I am reminded of a true story told to me many years ago by my good friend, Dr. Julius Krombach: When he was still practicing in Syracuse, he was consulted by an old-looking patient who was all hunched up, bent, and barely able to talk. "This is something terrible to look forward to when I get older," the doctor thought to himself. He soon found out, though, that the patient was only 59, while he, himself, was past 65.

While living in Syracuse I visited some of the local nursing homes. One time, I remember, a few of the elderly ladies had recently recovered from the flu but were showing signs of complete fatigue and exhaustion. Mrs. Kennedy, the proprietor, asked me to do something for the poor souls, and I remembered having learned in my student days about an injectable drug called Coramine, a circulatory stimulant. Well, once I administered the medication, the old ladies seemed to perk right up. Mrs. Kennedy was so impressed that she suggested that I go to Woodlawn Cemetery and give the same treatment to some of the "residents" there. I am sure that she overestimated me and my abilities.

Years later, I saw a sixty-some-year-old man on a home visit. The patient, Mr. S., was in terrible condition, had been vomitting continuously, and had lost a lot of weight. After I examined him I was sure that this man had a malignancy in his intestinal tract. He had refused hospitalization before, but I was able to convince him to be admitted immediately and be examined by Dr. Leon Berman, a most well-known Syracuse surgeon. Mr. S. was operated on, gained his weight back, and while visiting with Dr. Berman some time later, slapped the good doctor on the shoulder so hard that it hurt. Dr. Berman did not mind that at all; in fact he told me, "Whenever I feel a little depressed by the limits of surgery in some cases, I think of Mr. S., and my outlook brightens." He was an excellent surgeon, even a professor of surgery at Syracuse's Medical College, yet he did not rush into surgery when a medical solution was possible. He expressed this credo in his much-discussed article, "The Nonoperating Surgeon." Dr. Berman passed away quite a few years ago. His office is continued by his associates, Dr. Ernest Sarason and Dr. Daniel Burdick, and two young surgeons.

I bought a house at 1829 South Salina Street, on the south side of Syracuse. Our living quarters were upstairs, while the downstairs served as my office. As the house was quite spacious and rooms were hard to find, we rented apartment space to students from Syracuse University. Several of these tenants have done well in later life: Seymour Carren is in horticulture, and his wife Roslyn is an artist. I saw them again quite a few summers ago in Dallas. Ernest G. Beier and Ted Landsman, psychologists, both became university professors in their field. Joshua Goldberg is chairman of the physics department of Syracuse University and was elected president of Syracuse Friends of Chamber Music. About four or five years ago I met Manfred De Martino at the Syracuse-DeWitt Post Office after having not seen him for about twenty-five years. He had just finished his latest book, *Human Auto-Erotic Practices,* and is still professor of psychology at Syracuse's Onondaga Community College. Last, but not least, there is our former tenant, Ralph Golio, now a maintenance man at one of the local Howard Johnson establishments; he comes to the house whenever we need the services of a "handy-man."

Practice

It was not too difficult for me to start a new practice in Syracuse. First, it was close to Tully, so that many of my old patients were able to continue with me. Second, I continued to have office hours in Tully about twice a week for a while. Some of my colleagues in the city also asked me to make home visits for them in the beginning whenever they were unable to get away. One of these was my friend Dr. Robert Schwartz (Herta's obstetrician), who told me, "You will never become rich, but you will always make a living." How did he know that? He was right.

I was also registered with the police, and they called me for emergency care. Once, when I was called to a lady's house, the woman who opened the door for me exclaimed, "She is too sick to see anybody." After some explanation, she let me in.

Practice was not monotonous in Syracuse: blacks and whites, people of Irish, German, French, Spanish, and Italian heritage, Japanese war brides, Polish, Korean, and Vietnamese people—all were looking for relief from their ailments. "What do you think of us Irish," a patient once asked me, "electing a Jew Lordmayor of Dublin?" He meant, of course, Robert Briscoe, who was elected mayor of Dublin twice and who had appeared on talk shows and in lecture halls. Briscoe, who was played by Art Carney on a television program, tells a delightful story in his autobiography: He was reviewing the New York St. Patrick's Day parade in his mayoral robe when two Jewish women spotted him. "You see, this is Robert Briscoe, a Jew, who is Lordmayor of Dublin," one told the other. "Isn't that wonderful," the other one exclaimed. "And this could only happen in America!"

I was and still am in general practice with a special interest in psychosomatic disease. There is an old saying, "The general practitioner knows less and less about more and more, and the specialist knows more and more about less and less." In the fifties, a new specialty, family practice, arose. I did not feel that the new specialty was for me, and Dr. Hugo Stern, whose son-in-law is a well-known family practice specialist, agreed with me. It was during the McCarthy era, and I explained in jest to Dr. Krombach that I hesitated to join the Academy for Family Physicians as one never knew if a new organization might not be considered "subversive." Dr. Krombach, knowing that doctors in other specialties often felt that family practice was intrusive, answered, "By the specialist, probably."

In any case, the older I get, the less I feel able to take care of the whole family. For years I have not done any work in obstetrics, pediatrics, or orthopedics. I still am a general practitioner, a generalist, a primary physician. For the acutely ill patient, a visit to the generalist is the first line of defense. How often I have seen that a sick individual needs an excuse from work for her employer. Instead of going to her general practitioner, she gets an appointment with a specialist for a complete physical at a much later date, by which time her symptoms have left her. She still does not know what ailed her in the first place. Besides, with so many sub-specialties in existence, it is hard to know which specialist should have been chosen to diagnose the case. Yes, there will always be the need for the general practitioner, who diagnoses 90 percent of all the common and not-so-common diseases. I have to admit, though, that I am always willing to agree on and recommend consultation whenever a second, expert opinion would be beneficial. It is of the utmost importance for the patient that the referring physician receives a complete and detailed report from the consultant, so that he may sit down with the particular patient to intelligently discuss the patient's problem and allay his fears. Unfortunately, with all the necessary laboratory testing and other time-consuming research procedures, the specialist does not have the time to clear up the doubts and frustrations of the sick individual; that is up to the primary physician. Aside from private practice, I have taken care of Medicaid patients from the start of the Medicaid program. It is a rewarding experience to be able to treat the disadvantaged who are not able to afford private care for their hypertension, heart disease, stomach disorders, rheumatic diseases, depression and anxiety problems, or to afford exploratory surgery. True, the low fees leave much to be desired for the physicians, but the county and state departments for social services in New York State have always seen to it that the physician is reimbursed in proper time. Luckily, I have been able to get the consulting services of every kind of specialist for my patients in this program. Years ago, I apologized on the phone to proctologist Dr. Robert Curtiss for referring a Medicaid patient to him. "If you are good enough to accept it," he replied, "so am I, Heinz."

"Missionaries"

During the first years we lived in Syracuse, Herta and I took some vacations with our daughter Joan. I also went alone to New York State Medical Society meetings and to visit friends from my student days, and I learned a great deal about how other people still viewed the Jews.

My friend Herbert Neisser, who took the medical state board in Breslau with me, had a flourishing practice in Newport News, Virginia. I visited him one summer, and for some reason or other, the Virginia heat was very hard for me to take. The Neissers took me to dinner at the plush Newport News Hotel where a large sign was highly visible: "Air conditioned. Please keep your jackets on." I squirmed and squirmed until Annyce, Dr. Neisser's wife, advised me to hang my coat over the chair. I did, and enjoyed my dinner. I was also able to meet many physicians at a doctors' club, including Dr. Ernst Schweiger with his wife Herta, a friend and distant relative. He, a rabbi's son, practices in Portsmouth, Virginia. I shall never forget the story he told me about a patient of his, a fundamentalist Protestant minister: The clergyman noticed a picture of the physician's grandfather in the consultation room.

"You see the wrinkles on your grandfather's forehead?" he asked. "You see the sad expression in his face? He was not happy because he didn't recognize the Lord Jesus as his Savior. . . ."

"That he did not believe in Jesus as the Messiah was not the reason for his unhappiness," the doctor replied. "Because you people hunted and persecuted him, because you did not let him rest at night, he suffered so much that it showed in his facial expression."

The reverend thought and thought and finally answered, "You know, you have got something there."

It is odd but true that, since we came to the United States, we have been approached by Christian friends and strangers who try to convert us. While Siegmund Freud lived in exile in Britain until his death in 1939, he received numerous communications from all over the world urging him to get baptized. He was very touched by the concern of these good people, but he reaffirmed that he did not believe in "organized religion."

I have found that "missionaries" don't have senses of humor. One of those zealous women came to the house when Herta wasn't feeling too well. When Herta started to complain about some headaches, general achiness, tiredness, nervousness, and a host of other ailments, I jokingly blurted out, "Oh, my God, I cannot hear so much about illness!" The proselytizing woman looked at me with a stern face and inquired, "What kind of a doctor is he?" She never came to see me as a patient.

On one of our trips we visited Judith Sternberg-Newman, who lived with her husband Senek and children on a farm near Providence, Rhode Island. She had been a nurse at Breslau Jewish Hospital with Herta. We found her, like so many other people, through *Aufbau,* the German Jewish weekly. Judith was arrested by the Nazis in 1942, when she was the pediatric chief nurse at Breslau Jewish Hospital. Ten thousand Jews were rounded up for a transport to Auschwitz, and she was one of thirty-eight who "lived" through the ordeal. She lost her mother, three brothers, two sisters, and her young fiance in the Auschwitz Holocaust. During my visit she showed me her diary, which had helped her to continue her life after the terrible tragedy she'd had to survive. She gave the manuscript to Exposition Press, which published her memoirs under the title *In the Hell of Auschwitz.* I had encouraged Judith to have the book published without regard to sales possibilities, and hers was one of the first publications of its kind to come out.

Judith's little volume has been quoted by many authors, including Reeve Robert Brenner in *The Faith and Doubt of Holocaust Survivors* and by Otto Friedrich in his understanding article, "The Kingdom of Auschwitz," from the September 1981 *Atlantic* magazine. Since the appearance of Judy's memoirs, many similar stories about the Holocaust have come out. It took the victims more than two decades to overcome their denial and break their silence. *The Survivor in Us All* is the title of a recent book on the subject written by Erna Rubenstein, wife of a Syracuse physician. Her family was driven from their family in Poland; Erna lost her parents and younger brother, but she was miraculously able to escape Auschwitz with her four sisters. It is a very moving book.

Well-meaning people might tell you that one must forgive and forget. The survivors will not forgive, nor can they forget the saintly victims, family, and friends whose only "crime" was that they were Jews.

I remember a David Susskind television show many years ago featuring reporter Howard Blum, who had written the book *Wanted: The Search for Nazis in America.* Another panel member was the elderly lawyer who had defended a woman who was a supervisor at concentration camps, including Ravensbruck, and who was responsible for the death and beatings of Jewish inmates. The woman immigrated to America after the war, married an American, and became a naturalized American citizen. She lived in Queens, New York, until her identity was discovered. She was then deported to Germany to face trial, and her lawyer complained bitterly about the Jews who, he said, were not ready to forgive in accordance with Christian love but instead acted according to the Old Testament's "an eye for an eye. . . ." He did not know, of course, that in Israel these strict rules actually referred to monetary compensation. If a court condemned to death one person in 70 years, the court was called a cruel one.

It is certainly hard to understand that, in a country of poets and thinkers, the Nazis were able to plan and execute a systematic extermination of the Jews. A few commentators have tried to convince the public that the number of victims has been highly exaggerated. Not six million Jews, they say, possibly a million and a half. Another gentleman, a professor of electrical engineering at an Illinois university, has declared that all the concentration camp horrors were, in reality, a hoax invented by Jewish propagandists. Two or three years ago, I watched the "Freeman Reports" on Cablenews. Sandy Freeman had two Polish Jewish Holocaust survivors on her show and was able to talk with the Illinois professor on a telephone hookup. Ms. Freeman asked the scientist if he would like to discuss the issue with these Auschwitz survivors, and his answer was, "I don't want to talk with them; they are highly emotional people, and they don't speak English well."

Then the woman survivor spoke up. "Do you hear me, Professor?" she asked. "You are a liar, and you may sue me."

"Did you understand her, Professor?" Ms. Freeman asked. He did. I don't know whether or not there was a lawsuit, but I do know what former German Chancellor Helmut Schmidt said in 1979, forty years after the start of the Second World War (my translation from German):

> The memory of Auschwitz will stay alive for generations in Europe, Israel, America, and other countries of the world, and must stay alive also with us in our own country. We have found many friends since, and one has confidence in us again. We are not condemned in all eternity, but we ought to know at the same time that the after-Hitler-era will never be over for us.

Voyage of the Damned

Through *Aufbau* I found my first and second cousins, the Spitz family, who live in the city of Toronto. They were also from Breslau. George Spitz, the father, had moved his family and his blouse factory from England, where they had originally emigrated, to Canada. Both George and his wife Vera have since passed away, but their son Eric and their daughter Uschi continue to live in that beautiful city with their own grown children and grandchildren. Eric married Inge, a German-Jewish girl from Berlin, while he was in England. His sister Uschi became the wife of Johnny Miller, who was born and raised in England.

It had not been easy for the Spitz family to get to the United Kingdom from Nazi Germany. It was in May of 1939 that the approximately one thousand German Jews who had been able to purchase visas for Cuba were on board the *St. Louis*, a luxury steamer sailing from Hamburg. Eric Spitz, 15 years old, his sister Uschi, and his mother Vera were on that boat, while father George had been admitted to Cuba a short time previously. The Nazis knew that the visas of those poor *St. Louis* refugees were invalid and that they never would be admitted to Cuba. Also, there were Gestapo agents and spies on the ship. The Nazis wanted to show the world that no country was going to help those poor Jews. The brave German captain Gustav Schroeder did his best to help his Jewish passengers, but to no avail. They were not allowed into Cuba, and, even though they were able to see the lights of Miami from the ship, President Roosevelt did not have the power to have them legally admitted to the United

States. The refugees were then sent to Belgium, France, Holland, and Great Britain. Soon afterward, Belgium, France, and Holland were overrun by the Nazis, and the majority of the *St. Louis* passengers perished in their countries of "refuge." Eric, Uschi, their mother, and about 250 others were lucky enough to find a home in England.

In 1974, thirty-five years after that tragic ocean trip, Gordon Thomas and Max Morgan Witts, two former British Broadcasting producers, wrote the book *Voyage of the Damned* about the *St. Louis*. They became emotionally drained as they interviewed former crew members and the few remaining Jewish survivors, for the book.

After the book's appearance, Eric and Uschi were interviewed by various Toronto newspapers. After all, they were and are the only *St. Louis* survivors in the city of Toronto.

In 1976, two years later, a movie came out based on and named after the refugees' story, also called *Voyage of the Damned*. Oscar Werner played an assimilated German-Jewish physician, and his beautiful wife was played by Faye Dunaway. The brave German captain Gustav Schroeder was acted magnificently by Max von Sydow. Many other well-known stars gave memorable performances. Eric and Uschi found the movie most authentic. Many film reviewers did not agree, though. They could not comprehend that the Nazi government could be so obsessed with the extermination of those poor Jewish people, whose only crime was their Jewishness. In the critics' opinion, all the scenes of harassment on this ill-fated liner surely must have been exaggerated or invented. I wanted to form my own opinion and asked Mel, my son-in-law, to view the motion picture with me. He agreed, but I had to promise to attend the premiere of *Rocky* with him the following week. We both had much praise for *Voyage of the Damned*. Although there was certainly much good acting in *Rocky,* when we left the movie house, after watching all those boxing matches, I couldn't help exclaiming: "This was an anticlimax!" And Mel concurred.

Eric met his beautiful wife Inge in London, and both came to Toronto in 1948. Her maiden name is Rosenthal, and she originally came from Berlin. When she was just about twelve years old, she and her younger sister Edith found refuge in a French camp, owned by Baron Edouard Rothschild, for young Jewish children. For a year and a half, during the German occupation of France, Inge and Edith had to hide and were lucky enough to be able to live in a convent under different names. In May of 1944, the sisters crossed the border into Switzerland. They spent two years at refugee camps in Geneva, Montreaux, Lausanne, and Lugano. In January 1946 the girls were finally reunited with their parents in London. There Inge met her husband-to-be Eric, and two years later they moved to Canada. Sister Edith, now Mrs. Rogers, came to Canada in 1949.

Herta and I have attended the marriages of Inge's three sons as well as the marriages of Eric's sister Uschi's two daughters in Toronto. Inge and Eric visit us in Syracuse about twice a year with their cousin Greta Lehman from New York. She also suffered a similar ordeal in Nazi Germany and is part of our family now.

When Inge was visiting us about five years ago, I was able to present her with a copy of Saul Friedlander's *When Memory Comes*. The author, now a professor of political science in Tel Aviv and Geneva, was born into an assimiliated Jewish family in Czechoslovakia in 1932 and was taken by his parents to France seven years later to escape the Nazi persecution. He was at a home for Jewish children first; later, when the warclouds drew nearer, he was placed in a Catholic boarding school. His parents perished in Auschwitz. Friedlander was raised a Catholic and excelled in his religious studies. Just as he was about to enter a seminary, he was asked by a kind, elderly priest, "Didn't your parents die at Auschwitz?" His answer was, as he remembers, "What is Auschwitz?" Gradually, he went back to his Jewish roots.

This reminds me of a similar case. Jean Marie Lustiger, son of Polish-Jewish immigrants, was baptized at the age of 14, was elevated to Archbishop of France, and eventually was made Cardinal by Pope John Paul in 1983. Still, he has never denied his Jewish heritage and considers himself a Jew, in disagreement with most of today's rabbis.

California

Since Lucy van der Linde's arrival in this country, we have gone to see our relatives in California on many occasions. Lucy's late husband, Gerry van der Linde, was of partial Jewish descent and became a member of the Jehovah's Witnesses sect in his later years. Some of their children and grandchildren (as well as great-grandchildren) are Jewish; others are Christian. Herta's late brother Herbert and his wife Paula, also deceased, owned Friedman's Furniture Factory in Los Angeles and are survived by a son and a daughter.

Herta has always been very close to her family, and at one point she persuaded me to take the California medical license examination so that we might move to the West. In Europe a physician is able to move from one state to another after passing the state board once. This is not the case in the United States.

The state licensing exams took several days, and one had to score at least 75 percent to pass. The first part consisted of preclinical subjects like anatomy, chemistry, and physiology, for which one "crammed" and which one could afford to forget afterward. I hated that, as I had so many more important things to do and had to take care of my medical practice. I never failed a clinical subject in my tests, and I finally scored between 71 and 72 percent. Then I read in the California state board instructions that the examiners were prepared to grant up to five percentage points, one for each year of medical practice. I wrote the authorities about that, and they replied that this particular law had since been repealed. I finally gave up trying to move west for many,

many reasons, and I have never regretted it.

One of my advisers in Los Angeles was a distant relative, Dr. Luc Lewin; I am still in touch with his widow, Ilse Lewin, who lives in Southern California. Another friend, Dr. Dante Lombardi, took and passed his medical state board in Sacramento. Although he received his California license, he practices with a group in New York City. We have been friends since we met in California more than twenty-five years ago, and he attended my seventieth birthday party with his wife Rose.

In recent years, when we have not been able to go to California, we have been visited in Syracuse by our California relatives. When I celebrated my seventieth birthday, we had four generations here from the sunshine state: Lucy, her daughter Ruth, her granddaughter Sabrina, and her five-year-old great-grandson Marci.

One year, Lucy's beautiful daughter Mary Ann, her Mexican-born husband Rudolf Bautista, and their daughter Monique dropped in on their way to see Mary Ann's son Jerry. He had graduated from Stanton University and was working toward his doctorate in chemical engineering at Princeton. While Mel, our son-in-law, drove our guests around the university section and other sites in Syracuse, Mary Ann asked me, "Uncle Heinz, do you ask your women patients about sex when they come to you? I think that is terrible." I told her that I would discuss it if they wanted to, but I also related to her a story that a lecturer at one of the psychiatric sessions of a New York Medical Society meeting told us: A family physician who was anxious to take a good history of one of his elderly women patients asked her, "Well, Mrs. Rothenberg, what do you think about sex?" "I'll tell you, Doc," she replied, "I think Saks is one of the finest stores on Fifth Avenue."

"I'll have to remember that," Mary Ann said. I don't believe she does.

Breakdown

Herta's sister Lucy, brother-in-law Gerry, and their five children had been able to join us in the United States in 1945. But my parents, my sister Kate, Herta's mother, her younger brother Erwin, and his wife and young child have never been heard from again. They perished in the Nazi Holocaust.

Herta had always been very close to her family, and it was most difficult for her to leave her elderly mother behind when we had to flee Germany in 1939 to save our own lives. I was busy with my patients and felt needed, but my wife had a much harder time forgetting our sad recent history. In the early 1950s, when our daughter Joan Suzanne was about seven or eight, her mother suffered a "nervous breakdown" with marked depressive features. Paul and Helen Halpin, our neighbors, took Joan into their home and took care of her during Herta's prolonged illness. And Dr. Arthur Fleiss, a professor of neurology and psychiatry, who hardly knew me, gave freely of his time and skill to help us in this emergency situation.

There are life situations in which even the strongest individual will break physically and mentally. After having lived as a Jew in Nazi Germany, having to be separated from and worried about loved ones left behind, and having to learn the terrible, unbelievable final truth—no one under such circumstances should have to apologize for suffering a "nervous breakdown."

It is true that post-war Germany has been paying restitution to surviving Nazi-victims to reimburse them in part for their sufferings. Herta still receives some restitution. The claimant is examined by a special consultant authorized by the German government who determines if there is a connection between the victim's present illness and the Nazi persecution. Some of these physician-experts readily agree that it is not surprising to find psychiatric illness among the survivors; what is surprising is that the number of these patients is much smaller than expected.

After Herta was somewhat improved, she and Joan stayed for many months at the home of Herta's brother Herbert in Los Angeles, while I tried to concentrate on my Syracuse medical practice. It was the late William Menninger who once declared that every psychiatric resident should have lived through a crisis in his own family to become a competent physician. I am qualified now in this respect; but no "crisis" should be necessary in the life of a doctor to prove his medical competence.

There is no doubt that the continued practice of medicine helped me more than anything to live through all the difficult times. I also read then (and again recently) Viktor Frankl's *Man's Search For Meaning*. The author, a professor of psychiatry and neurology at the University of Vienna and guest lecturer at several American universities, is the founder of logotherapy, a technique of searching for meaning in life. For three years he was imprisoned by the Nazis at Auschwitz and other concentration camps; he lost his young wife and most of his other relations; he saw fellow prisoners around him shot and did not know from one moment to the next whether he himself would be struck down. His prison garb torn, his feet wounded, he also lost a valuable manuscript on which he had worked for a very long time. Yet, he managed to survive by imagining how, after his liberation, he would write about the psychological changes in himself and the other inmates. He found meaning in his suffering, and as long as a person finds meaning in his life, he has the will to survive. One does not have to be religious to be helped by logotherapy. For some reason, many psychiatric textbooks don't mention Dr. Frankl. But, one book in which he is mentioned, the beautiful one-volume *Theory and Practice of Psychiatry* by Redlich and Freedman, says that Frankl's teachings could be as theological as they are psychological.

Another book that helped me a great deal is *When Bad Things Happen to Good People*. Written fairly recently, it tries to explain, in simple language, how modern people can go on living after tragedies have befallen them. It was written by Rabbi Harold Kushner, although it is not a specifically Jewish book, and it spent over a year on the hardcover best seller list.

The author's son Aaron died at an early age of progeria, a rare disease, as his doctors had predicted. All the consolations the rabbi received from members of his congregation were not good enough for him. He could not accept the dictum that the death of his young son was somehow an act of God, that God was trying to teach him something or to punish him for something. He believes in a God who will ultimately make the good triumph over the bad but who is not all-powerful. We who were brought up in the Jewish tradition know, of course, that God could not be all-powerful as long as man has a free will. The Jewish theologian Richard L. Rubenstein said in his book *After Auschwitz* that it is obscene to believe in the traditional God of reward and punishment who somehow used the Nazis and S. S. guards as instruments to punish the Jewish people. Other religious philosophers, like Eliezer Berkovits and Emil Fackenheim, found different explanations for the hiding of the Deity. But Kushner, by quoting Hiob and other biblical sources, was able to get the attention of a more general audience regardless of their religion or affiliation, with all their smaller and larger tragedies.

Aside from reading his book and seeing him on the "Phil Donahue Show," I listened to Rabbi Kushner speak at two local synagogues. The lectures were open to the general public. The first time, I went with my son-in-law Mel to Temple Adath Yeshurun, where the speaker was introduced by his friend, Rabbi Charles Sherman. Kushner was a powerful orator, expounding the ideas in his book in clear, understandable fashion. In the discussion which followed, Dr. David Jakubowski, a general practitioner of Polish-Jewish heritage who had lost many of his loved ones during the Holocaust, declared that, after forty years of wrestling with confusion, some of his problems had become clearer to him because of this lecture. He recited the words that had been found on the walls of a cellar in Cologne where Jews had been hiding from the Nazis. "I believe in the sun, even when it is not shining; I believe in love, even when feeling it not; I believe in God, even when He is silent." Dr. Jakubowski received almost as much applause as did the main speaker.

Inasmuch as my daughter Joan had not been able to attend Kushner's first lecture, I took her along to the second lecture about three months later at Temple Beth Shalom, where Rabbi Daniel Jezer introduced Rabbi Kushner. (Joan had attended Central High School in Syracuse, where all her classmates and friends were non-Jewish. Despite the many Jewish books in my library and the closing of my office on the Jewish holidays and even her attendance of Jewish Sunday school classes, it took her a long time to find her Jewish identity. But one day, she went with her friend Judy Windsor to see *The Ten Commandments,* a movie whose main character, Moses, is played by Charlton Heston. She has had no problem with her identity since.) We went to Temple Beth Shalom with our good friend Linda Chew Cantor, daughter of a non-Jewish mother and a Jewish father. I sat down in the crowded auditorium and realized that I was not wearing a skullcap in this conservative synagogue. I told this to Joan, who was in the row behind me, but was assured by a delightful young Protestant minister sitting next to her, "I don't wear a yarmulke, either, and I haven't been thrown out yet." After the lecture we shook hands with some very pleasant Catholic nuns, and the young minister behind me gave me his opinion of the speaker. "You know, for me the man is a Christian," he said. For me, of course, he is a Jew. What is it that makes us separate?

The personal stories of three Jewish personalities come to mind. There is the writer Paul Cowan, author of *An Orphan in History* and son of very assimilated Jewish parents. He opposed the Vietnam War and, in protesting, met and became a friend of Father Daniel Berrigan. The priest caused him to search for a more meaningful religious life, but Cowan was not able to believe as the priest did; the belief in Jesus separated them. Cowan searched for his roots and eventually joined the Jewish community with his wife Rachel, who came from a Unitarian background.

Generation Without Memory is the title of a book by Anne Roiphe. A few years ago she wrote an article in the *New York Times* about how she, despite being "nominally Jewish," has celebrated Christmas with a decorated tree for many years. The article, called "Christmas Comes to a Jewish Home," got a flood of critical responses. These responses might have influenced her to write the beautiful small volume *Jewish Journey in Christian America,* describing her search for Jewish values.

Gerald S. Strober, who came from a very assimilated Jewish family, had no Jewish education to speak of. When he was eighteen, he was given a New Testament tract, read it, converted to Christianity, and entered the fundamentalist Protestant Moody Bible Institute in Chicago. Gradually, cracks appeared in his belief during the many years of his involvement with Christian evangelism. He was greatly influenced by the Jewish philosopher Franz Rosenzweig and also by the Canadian-Jewish scholar Emil Fackenheim, who demanded in his writings that the Jews should preserve their Jewish heritage "in order not to allow Hitler any posthumous victories." Strober returned to Judaism in 1974, published "My Life As A Christian" in the June 1982 edition of *Commentary* magazine, and he hopes to write at greater length about his return to the Jewish community.

... Always a Jew

I, myself, who was lucky enough to get out of Nazi Germany, always knew that I was Jewish. Being persecuted as Jews, it was up to us to find out what our place in history was and is. Moses Mendelssohn, a famous Jewish philosopher of the nineteenth century, translated the Hebrew Bible into German and tried to promote the assimilation of Jews into German culture. His grandson, Felix Mendelssohn Bartholdy, the well-known composer and director of church music, had been baptized as a child. Still, the next generation of the Mendelssohns was considered Jewish by the Third Reich. There is no getting away from it. Even now, well-meaning friends (or are they?) give us their advice about solving the "Jewish question"; they feel that the Jews should intermarry and completely assimilate. Well, if I had been a Nazi, I would be anxious to break with my past. But, as a Jew, what reason do I have to give up my heritage and Judaism? Siegmund Freud, one of my heroes, found in Protestant minister Oskar Pfister one of his most devoted psychoanalytic pupils. When Freud, an agnostic, secular Jew, wrote the clergyman and asked why the world had to wait for a "godless Jew" to devise psychoanalysis, he received a most beautiful reply from Pfister. "In the first place you are not a Jew, which my boundless admiration for Amos, Isaiah, the author of Job and the prophets makes me greatly regret, and in the second place you are not so godless since he who lives for truth lives in God and he who fights for the freeing of love dwelleth in God."

Many years ago I heard Rabbi Samuel Goldenson, rabbi

emeritus of New York's Temple Emanuel at that time, say that an atheistic Jew is still considered a Jew. He was guest-lecturing at Syracuse's Temple Concord, and I saw him at my office for a minor medical problem during his stay. He quoted from the Talmud, "Better that they [the Jews] abandon me, but follow my laws," and said that the Talmud adds that, by practicing Jewish laws, the Jews will return to their God, who is the universal God. Actually, there are not many Jewish "atheists." As Elie Wiesel, one of the foremost Jewish survivors of the Holocaust, declares, "The Jew may love God, or he may fight with God, but he may not ignore God." I have never had any problem with the Jewish God idea. It is easy to agree with the German philosopher Immanuel Kant: "Two things fill me with awe. The starry heavens and the sense of moral responsibility in man." It is difficult, of course, to believe in the traditional God after the horrors of the Holocaust. A dialogue often repeated, according to Francine Klagsbrun in *Voices of Wisdom,* was the question, "At Auschwitz, where was God?" and the answer, "Where was Man?"

Or as it says in *Ethics of the Fathers,* "The reward for a good deed is another good deed and the reward for a transgression is another transgression."

The guide for the Jewish people in relation to God and humanity has always, since the beginning of Judaism, been the Hebrew Bible. When the Jews became dispersed, the biblical laws were discussed, adjusted to the living conditions at the given time, and transmitted to us as the "oral law" in the form of the Mischnah and Talmud. It is surprising that the opinions of the rabbis about two thousand years ago concerning contraception, abortion, artificial insemination, euthanasia, and autopsy are very similar to our modern ethical discussions.

One of the newer Jewish movements, the Society for Humanistic Judaism, does not recognize the supremacy of the Bible. The founder, Rabbi Sherwin Wine, who wrote the book *Humanistic Judaism* a few years ago, feels that for the humanistic Jew the study of Einstein, Freud, and Herzl. is preferable to the study of the Bible, and that the study of Fromm's works will do more for us than the study of Rabbi Akiba. I wrote a letter to the then editor of *The Humanist* magazine expressing my disagreement with humanistic Judaism and the book. It seems to me that there is no real difference between "Jewish" humanism and humanism per se. The so-called Jewish humanists pay hardly any attention to the most profoundly Jewish experience and heritage—the Holocaust. Each Jewish person must find a way to come to grips with this tragedy and decide whether to continue in or reject his Jewish faith. By ignoring this issue, there ceases to be anything especially Jewish about the Jewish humanist.

I had a Jewish-Conservative background. It is difficult to explain the differences between the three branches of Judaism: Orthodox, Conservative, and Reform. I remember well that many years ago Rabbi Irwin Hyman of Temple Adath Yeshurun declared before a huge audience: "I am an Orthodox rabbi who heads a Conservative temple with a Reform congregation." I was never able to identify with the Orthodoxy and its excommunication of Jewish personalities like Uriel Acosta and Baruch Spinoza who critiqued the Bible and had original ideas about God. I now belong to Temple Society of Concord, a Reform synagogue. The gulf between Conservative and Reform Judaism is not that great, and I have seen Jewish persons change easily from one branch to the other if they have to move to another community that does not have the synagogue of their preference nearby. But, in modern Israel, marriages between Conservative and Reform Jews are not recognized by the leading Orthodox rabbis there.

I am disturbed by contradictions in religious teachings. It seems implausible to me that the same God who accepts animal sacrifices from his people also spoke the eternal words through his prophet Micah: "He had told you, O man, what is good, and what the Lord requires of you. Only to do justice and to love goodness and to walk modestly with your God." (I have remembered that quote since the first time I heard it in Adlai Stevenson's acceptance speech for the Democratic presidential nomination.) It is my firm conviction also that leaders of nations cannot be expected to reach an agreement to find a basis for peace while Arab and Jewish leaders are claiming that the same land is promised to them by God.

Even the Orthodox Jews have a healthy attitude toward sex. They have never believed that sex is permitted for procreation only. Their attitude differs sharply from the apostle Paul's, who pronounced, "It is better to marry than to be aflame with passion." Yet, the orthodox of all religions even today consider masturbation an evil, a cardinal sin. It was not too long ago that children, adolescents, and adults were warned of the terrible physical and mental "dangers" of the habit, and many, most sensitive people were driven to suicide. Karl Menninger, the famous psychiatrist, tells us in his excellent *Whatever Became of Sin?* that these medical and moral attitudes changed overnight some time after the turn of the century. He also said that after finding out that the solitary "sin" of masturbation, committed by about one hundred percent of the people, could no longer be considered a sin, many people thought that nothing must be a sin anymore and threw overboard all the other transgressions like lying, cheating, stealing, and even murder.

Sex education concerning homosexuality, lesbianism, adolescent sex, and teen-age pregnancy is frowned upon by orthodox-fundamentalist-Christian preachers. Dr. Sol Gordon, professor of child and family studies at Syracuse University, is invited each year by Dr. Frank Oski, chief of pediatrics, to give a talk before the doctors about teen-age sex education or a similar topic. In spite of the fact that he warns in his writings against sexual affairs between adolescents—because of their lack of maturity—his books are called "pornographic" by fundamentalists. Dr. Mary Steichen-Calderone, who has long been active in the field of sex information and is the author of *The Family Book About Sexuality*—a very meritorious lady—has been attacked for years from many orthodox pulpits for her "immorality."

As I have already mentioned, I belong to the Reform branch of Judaism and have been a member of the liberal Temple Society of Concord in Syracuse for many years. How does the Reform Jew interpret the Hebrew Bible? Rabbi Ronald Gittelsohn writes in his widely read *Love, Sex, and Marriage: A Jewish View:*

[Today, Jews] must respect our traditions without necessarily following them. Most of the ethical concepts of Judaism are at least as valid today as when they were first conceived by our ancestors. In some areas, however, because we have knowledge that was unavailable to them, it becomes necessary to revise or even discard their judgment.

In 1981, the first Reform Jewish Bible Commentary, *The Torah, A Modern Commentary,* edited by Rabbi W. Gunter Plaut, appeared in print. Plaut completed his law studies in Germany; but, influenced by the impact of the Nazi persecution, he studied for the rabbinate after he'd immigrated to the States. He had his first pulpit in Minnesota and eventually was called to the reformed Holy Blossom Temple in Toronto where he is active as rabbi emeritus now. His commentary has been acclaimed by Conservative Jewish scholars as well, like Professor Robert Gordis. Plaut—in contrast to the fundamentalists—writes in his introduction that:

The Torah is a human book composed by men. The Torah is a book about man's understanding of and experience with God. The Torah is ancient Israel's distinctive record of its search for God . . . a people's search for and meeting with God. . . . There ought to be something special about it. For over two and one half millennia the Torah has been the keystone of Jewish life, the starting point of Christendom and the background of Islam.

My association with the Reform synagogue never did prevent me from attending important Jewish events that were held at one of the other congregations. Harold Kushner's lectures about belief in God when "bad things happen to good people" were given at the Conservative temples Adath Yeshurun and Beth Shalom. Just the other night I went to the Orthodox Temple Beth El, whose spiritual leader is Rabbi David Sheinkopf, to attend a Holocaust Commemoration. One speaker at this event was Robert Clary, a French-Jewish concentration camp survivor who lost thirteen members of his immediate family to the Nazi terror. He has been known to the American public as an actor in the television show

"Hogan's Heroes." For the past three years, this wonderful speaker has been traveling around the country talking about the Holocaust—which he previously had been trying to forget—because of the "revisionists" who deny that there ever was a Holocaust. It was heartwarming to see such a large part of the non-Jewish community participating in this memorable event. Lutheran Bishop Edward Perry read from the Book of Ezekiel. Father Frank Haig, brother of the former Secretary of State Alexander Haig and president of LeMoyne College, was among the numerous guests, as was Mrs. Dorothy Rose, Executive Director of the Syracuse Area Interreligious Council. Bishop Frank Harrison addressed the capacity crowd and showed how important it is for human beings to stand up and be counted when evil seems to triumph in the world. He put into his own words the famous quote by Pastor Martin Niemöller, and said:

> At first, the Nazis went after the Jews, but I was no Jew, and I didn't speak up. Then they went after the Catholics, but I was no Catholic and remained silent. Then they went after the trade unions, but I was no trade unionist and did not say anything. Finally, they came after me, and there was nobody left to speak out anymore.

History of Jews in Syracuse

Syracuse is one of about twenty-five cities in the United States with an Interreligious Council, a meeting ground of Catholics, Protestants, Jews, Moslems, and followers of the Baha'i faith. Rabbi Theodore Levy, senior rabbi of Temple Concord, who is assisted by Rabbi Lawrence Schlesinger, was one of the founders and was first president of the Interreligious Council.

Just recently Temple Society of Concord celebrated its 145th anniversary, and Rabbi Emeritus Benjamin Friedman was honored on the occasion of his nintieth birthday at that same time. It was Rabbi Friedman who, over fifteen years ago, had encouraged Bernard G. Rudolph, a retired retail jeweler, to write a history of the Syracuse Jews. I first heard about the book, called *From a Minyan to a Community*, from Kathleen Niles, a young school teacher who had graduated from high school with Joan. She had typed the manuscript for Mr. Rudolph, and Syracuse University sponsored the publication. Naturally, as a member of the Syracuse Jewish community for the greater part of my life, I enjoyed searching through the book, and I found many interesting historical facts: Two leading Syracuse physicians, both born in 1857, were Dr. Henry Elsner, an internist, and Dr. Nathan Jacobson, a surgeon. Both happened to be members of Temple Society of Concord, were teaching at the Syracuse College of Medicine, and were in leading staff positions at Syracuse's St. Joseph Hospital.

Another interesting story is that of engineer Jacob X. Cohen, who designed the sewage disposal system for the city. It was hailed as "one of the most advanced achievements of sanitary engineering in this country." He had a good Jewish education and, despite his successful career as an engineer, decided in 1925 to study for the rabbinate. He later joined Dr. Stephen S. Wise as associate rabbi of New York City's Free Synagogue. He was encouraged in all this by Rabbi Benjamin Friedman of Syracuse. Cohen's biography, written by his widow, is entitled *Engineer of the Soul.*

One of the most famous American physicians was the late Samuel Rosen. He was born in Syracuse in 1897, and I learned about him first through Rudolph's book. He devised an operation, the stapedectomy, through which he helped thousands and thousands of otosclerotic (progressively deafening) patients to hear again. In 1956 he received the highest citation for original work in medicine from the American Medical Association, and one year later received a prestigious award from the University of Bologna. In 1964, Dr. Rosen was given the highest alumni award of Syracuse University by Chancellor William Tolley. Up to the time of his death in 1982, he remained consulting otologist at New York's Mount Sinai Hospital. He traveled extensively—to China, Russia, Japan, Africa, England, and many other European countries—to demonstrate his innovative ear surgery. He did the same at Cairo Medical College where he had a ninety-minute talk with the then Egyptian president Nasser. According to newspaper reports, Nasser said, "I am very grateful to you for coming here to help my people." Dr. Rosen answered, "Thank you, but I am surprised I was invited. I am Jewish, you know." Nasser replied, "We know that, too, but your work is above race or country; actually you doctors are the best diplomats." On his second trip to Israel, in 1960, he demonstrated his surgical skill again and was told by Prime Minister David Ben Gurion, "I am very pleased that you went to the Arab countries to teach them, as you did us. This is very good for everyone."

In one of two articles in the *Medical Tribune,* Dr. Arthur Sackler, international publisher, refers to his two good friends, both named "Sam": the one, Sam Levenson, who told funny stories to make people happy in his own special way, and the other, Sam Rosen, who enabled those people to hear the stories.

In the article of June 6, 1973, Dr. Sackler also spoke highly of the wonderfully written *Autobiography of Dr. Samuel Rosen.* As I was quite impressed with the story of the illustrious Syracuse ear surgeon, I searched in vain for an essay about Dr. Rosen in the sixteen-volume *Encyclopedia Judaica,* published by Keter in Jerusalem and printed by the Macmillan Company in the United States. I wrote to Professor Louis Rabinowitz, the associate editor, who confirmed that Samuel Rosen should have been included in the original *Encyclopedia.* He assured me that an article of mine about him would appear in the 1974 *Year Book.* It did, and it was reprinted in the 1982 *Dicennial Volume.* When I informed Dr. Rosen that my article about him would appear in the 1974 *Encyclopedia Judaica Year Book,* the gentleman with the many honors answered me:

> Dear Dr. Hartmann:
>
> What a fine person to have taken the time to write to *Encyclopedia Judaica* about me. I am happy at what you did primarily because it is so uncommon to find one as understanding and sensitive. I therefore feel enriched by your human act—*Encyclopedia* or not.
>
> With best wishes,
> Sam Rosen

A short time later, I sent him an extra copy I had of B. G. Rudolph's book, which he apparently had never seen.

Michael

I have digressed from the problems of my own family, and I have to return, remembering the words of Socrates, "An unexamined life is not worth living." The reader will recall Herta's emotional illness. Under the skillful guidance of Dr. Arthur Fleiss, her psychiatrist, and with the passage of time, her symptoms lessened gradually. So, we were overjoyed when, on November 9, 1954, our son Michael was born. His birth weight was eight pounds, five ounces, and his muscles seemed very strong. He started to make talking noises, so our friend Briggi was convinced that Michael would make progress well. Briggi was our tenant on South Salina Street at that time. She had stayed with us since the day when, while looking for a room, she saw Joan playing on the porch and said to her companion: *"Das ist aber ein huebsches Maedchen!"* (Look, that is a pretty girl!) She paid us one week's rent, continued to be our tenant, and we have been friends ever since. Joan, age eleven and a half at the time, could not believe that she had a baby brother. "Pinch me," she said. Our pediatrician friends were Drs. Robert Schwartz and Fred Roberts, and later Drs. Walter Charles, Arthur Stockman, and George Starr. "How is your shiny little boy?" Dr. Roberts would ask when my wife would call him to ask a question. We were extremely happy.

Like every baby, Michael was given the DPT vaccine to protect against diphtheria, pertussis (whooping cough), and tetanus. It was after the second triple-vaccine injection that Michael developed a high fever one night. Afterward, he failed to thrive, and he suffered from small seizures. He was hospitalized and was seen in consultation by Dr. Stanley Batkin, a professor of neurosurgery, and Dr. Julius Richmond, chairman of the Upstate Medical Center pediatrics department (he also held the post of U.S. Surgeon General at the start of the 1980s). Their diagnosis was encephalitis. They also gave us a bad prognosis. It was their consensus that Michael was "retarded" and would never develop normally. He stopped having convulsive seizures for about one year while under the influence of a small amphetamine medication, but they returned. Many, many pediatricians and other specialists have worried about Michael since! Once, during the first years of his illness, he was hospitalized at the old Syracuse City Hospital with a severe feverish disease. He was quite dehydrated, and it was Dr. Paul F. Wehrle who took it upon himself to force-feed Michael with chocolate milk. For years now, Dr. Wehrle has been professor of pediatrics at the USC School of Medicine and pediatric director of the Los Angeles County Medical Center.

Soon after Michael became ill, Dr. Schwartz, who had headed Michael's pediatric group, moved with his family to Florida. He suffered from heart disease and was hoping that the mild southern climate might be beneficial to him. We kept in contact, and one day he notified me that he was going to visit his remaining family in Syracuse in the near future and wished to see Michael during that time. I picked him up at the home of his brother, attorney Barney Schwartz, and our first stop was at the Jewish Home for the Aged, where one of the nurses gave him an injection for his cardiac condition. After that, on our way to see Michael, we were stopped at each corner by his many friends, who wished him well. "You know," Dr. Schwartz told me, "if it would not have been for the hard winters in Syracuse, I just as well would have stayed here." I brought Michael from his upstairs bedroom to my downstairs office, as the doctor's condition didn't permit him to climb the stairs. We discussed Michael's illness and the prognosis. "Whoever has a child like this," Dr. Schwartz told me, "his life is changed." He remembered instantly, though, that my life had changed already under the influence of Nazi Germany. When he passed away a short time later, I sent my condolences to his widow. She replied, "Bob always considered you one of his friends." It made me feel a little better.

On the advice of our Syracuse pediatrician, Dr. Frederick Roberts, we got in touch with Dr. Sidney Carter, head of pediatric neurology at New York's Columbia-Presbyterian Hospital, and had Michael admitted there for further evaluation. As Dr. Carter had to be out of the city, he referred us to his associate, Dr. Arnold Gold. Michael received a thorough medical checkup from Dr. Gold and his staff and was started on anticonvulsive medication for the first time. It is a great teaching hospital, but, surprisingly, there then existed no warmth or feeling in the various offices of that big institution. It seemed to me that some of the lady employees considered it their main task to prevent distraught parents from visiting their ill children. I hope that at this time a more kind and humane attitude prevails. Also on Dr. Roberts's advice, I sent a piece of an electro-encephalogram (brain-wave tracing) for evaluation to Dr. Frederick Gibbs, the famous neurologist in Chicago. Dr. Gibbs was kind enough to answer promptly, but the EEG tracing was not conclusive, and we had to continue to search for specialistic help from the Syracuse medical community.

As mentioned before, Michael's illness followed the administration of his second triple-vaccine shot. I remembered immediately from the medical literature that among thousands and thousands of immunizations, a small number of babies might get a form of whooping cough instead of the desired protection. The situation was the same in the case of the first Salk polio vaccinations, from which many young children became paralyzed or died, or, more recently, as when some adults showed major neurological complications as a result of the government-sponsored swine flu immunization. At the time, many people urged me to make a legal claim against the manufacturer of DPT vaccine so that Michael would be reimbursed and not be dependent on our support (we were not and are not rich) and inadequate insurance payments all of his life. There were three reasons why I never considered going to court: The first and most important reason was that I didn't want to get the doctors involved; they were not to blame as it could have happened to any physician who used that particular batch of vaccine. The second reason is "denial," a psychiatric term implying that I felt that such a bad thing just could not happen to me, a doctor, who (in my own opinion, at least) did not do too many bad things. Whenever our pediatricians or neurological consultants predicted that Michael would not develop normally and would be retarded all of his life, we just did not believe it. We felt that time would prove them wrong. The third reason, last but not least, was my resolution to do all I could for our boy and not to spend days in court when I was needed at home to give my son constant medical attention.

Michael is thirty-two years of age as of this writing. We still get medical advice from Dr. Roberts and his pediatric group. If and when hospitalization becomes necessary, an internist—according to hospital regulations—has to supervise Michael's care during his hospital stay. Dr. Donald Woolfolk helped us with medical care, and, now that he is in North Carolina, Dr. Paul Kronenberg helps us. Many neurologists, most connected with the Syracuse University Upstate Medical Center, have followed Michael right along: Dr. Arthur Ecker, Dr. William Wright, Dr. John Wolf (author of *Practical Neurology* and *Mastering Multiple Sclerosis*), and Dr. James Yurdin.

For years now, Michael has been on dilantin and mysoline medication. Still, about once a week, I must be up with him because he suffers a convulsion during the night. Blood levels of the drugs are checked at certain intervals; but, if the dose of the anticonvulsants is too low, seizures are prone to occur, and, if too high, toxic symptoms may occur. Up with me during the night at these times is Eleene Seeber, who has been living with us for more than twenty-five years. She loves Michael, and he loves her. She can do more for him than other women with better, more specialized educations can do. Also, we have daily help from several "home aides," so we are able to manage. And what fine people we've met because of Michael—as the majority of these aides served with such great devotion! One lady, Mrs. Genevieve Magen, a Jehovah's Witness, unfortunately passed away due to some rapidly progressive disease. We felt terribly sad then, and we shall always remember her loyalty and friendship. From all different backgrounds these people came: Catholic, Mormon, Pentecostal, black, and white, all united in their love for and desire to help Michael. There is Barbara Lillis, dependable and loyal; lively Jean Knighton, who always can make him laugh, even if he does not feel quite up to it; and Zywia Szwej, a young Polish lady who shows a keen interest in music, as does Michael. Twice a year, one or the other of these ladies accompanies him when he attends a dinner and concert sponsored by the Association for Retarded Children. There he meets his friends Michael Sagar and Clifford Gould and many other young adults who suffer some kind of brain damage, although the cause frequently differs. Michael moves joyfully back and forth in his wheelchair when he likes some of the dance music. But tears come if the band plays a sad melody.

Due to receiving continuous dilantin medication, Michael developed a severe gingivitis, so that his teeth became infected and had to be extracted by dental surgeons David Kennedy and Eric Pettit. Without teeth, he is unable to pronounce words as well as he once could. Still, he can make himself understood. If he would like to see a special television program, "The Lawrence Welk Show," "Ralph Emory," Johnny Cash on the Nashville network, or Jerry Lewis on the "Muscular Dystropy Telethon," he has a sense of timing and shows us in the *T.V. Guide* what program he wants to see. He needs help in walking. But, we can learn from him. Whenever we raise our voices, arguing about our time schedule for the day, he points a finger at one of us (mostly at Herta) and says, "Mean," and we quiet right down. On the other hand, if he likes somebody, even a well-meaning stranger, he might take his or her hand and puts it against his cheek. People are usually touched by this. We still have a picture of Michael with Denise D'Ascenzio, beautiful weather girl of the local ABC station, who's now in St. Louis. She looked so surprised when he took her hand to express his appreciation of her interest in him as a "different" human being. The other networks, like the local CBS station, have paid attention to Michael as when, for example, we gave a party for Eleene on her fiftieth birthday, several years ago. Patients still remember it and mention it to me. At this party for Eleene, Michael was also a guest of honor, and I was interviewed about Michael by the television network.

I am reminded of another television appearance of mine, close to ten years ago. It was a very hot summer, and one Sunday I received a phone call at about 9:30 A.M. from Stu Kellogg, a local ABC broadcaster. He asked if he could question me about heat exhaustion and heatstroke for the Sunday night news show. And he asked when it would be convenient for me.

"Maybe noon?" I asked.

"We are close to you, at Shoppingtown. Is it possible to come over to your home at 11?"

"O.K.," I said.

"Maybe we could come right away?"

"O.K.," I answered again.

When I came upstairs to our living room and informed Herta about the impending visit, she was surprised. Of course she wanted to clean the house, and I had not even thought of her herniated disk. She used a broom and pail and other tools to make our living room as respectable as she possibly could in that short time. A few minutes later, Stu Kellogg arrived with his cameraman. He looked at the house and yard and noticed the round table with an umbrella and two chairs on our front lawn. "Why don't we sit down and talk right under the umbrella?" he asked. It worked out fine. But, all that hard work in the living room was for nothing.

Michael does not get out very much, and television plays a big part in his life. For years he has been interested in musical programs, news, and comedy on all the major networks. The local affiliates of NBC, CBS, and ABC have always sent him pictures from their highly-rated shows as well as photos of their local celebrities. As the Syracuse ABC station is located only a short distance from our home, Joan took Michael there and introduced him personally to its news panel: Bud Hedinger, Ron Wood, and Mary McCombs. Bud Hedinger got a very good offer to be a television newscaster in Orlando, Florida. Before he left, he gave a special greeting to Michael over the air during his weather forecast. A few days later, he mailed Michael three autographed photographs of himself and enclosed the following heartwarming letter, dated February 25, 1986:

Dear Mike,

You and your family are very special people and I want you to know how much I'll miss you after we move to Florida.

Your sister thought you might enjoy a few pictures, so here they are! Best wishes to you for continued happiness. I'll never forget you.

Sincerely,
Bud Hedinger

The lives of so many people have been touched by our "special child."

Atonement

Tradition tells us that in the ten days between Rosh Hashanah, the Jewish New Year, and Yom Kippur, the Day of Atonement, the Jew has to mend his ways. I had explained to our friend Briggi, who did not know many Jewish people in her small hometown in Germany, that the Jew cannot expect forgiveness for an injustice to another human being unless the two have first straightened the matter out between themselves. I told her the following story: Two Jewish former friends met each other shortly before the Jewish New Year's day.

"Listen," one said to the other, "I know we have not been kind to each other for the past year. But let bygones be bygones. Let us forgive each other. And I wish you everything that you wish me."

"You see," the other retorted, "Now you start again!"

It is not only people from European countries who lack information about Jews and Judaism. In 1969, when I moved from South Salina Street to an office in the former Medical Arts Building, I shared the waiting room with Dr. John W. Pennock. When I informed his delightful secretary, Mrs. Terry Sposato, that I just had celebrated the Jewish New Year, she asked if we had gone out for a good dinner to celebrate. I assured her that that was not the idea of the Jewish New Year. "On the contrary," I explained, "We have to remember what we did wrong in the previous year and resolve to do better and to be better in the coming year." And you know what she answered? "I don't think you have got to worry too much there. . . ." Whenever I wonder whether I have done the right thing on a certain day, I think of that statement, and it gives me a little lift.

I have recently read a beautiful little article written by Mary Hedglon for the *Syracuse Herald Journal*. Shortly before Yom Kippur in 1984, she interviewed the one percent of Jews among the approximately 1700-man prison population of the nearby Auburn maximum security correctional facility. Actually, "less than one percent" of the prison inmates attend the weekly services, according to Mary Hedglon, which are led by Rabbi Laurence Schlesinger, Associate Rabbi of the Reform Temple Society of Concord. The Jewish prisoners are accused of the same crimes as their Gentile fellow-prisoners: robbing banks, shooting policemen, and murdering civilians. The "most famous member of the congregation" is a Jewish inmate who earned his law degree while in prison. He works as a lawyer for the other prisoners, and he still argues his own case. I like his sense of humor even among these tragic circumstances: He was going to attend Yom Kippur services and to fast on the Day of Atonement. As he explained to the interviewer, "Considering prison food, fasting on Yom Kippur is a blessing. . . ."

On a first night of Rosh Hashanah, in the 1960s, Herta and I were driving on East Castle Street, anxious to be on time for Rosh Hashanah services. I noticed a group of young black people sitting on the steps of an old house, and one of them approached my car while I was waiting for the stop light to turn green. He asked for a cigarette light. I replied that I was a nonsmoker, and Herta motioned for me to roll up the window and to disregard the stop light. I saw her point, and continued on. Our car was soon bombarded with glass bottles. The "safety" glass from the shattered windshield hit my eyes, and we ended up at the Crouse Irving Memorial Hospital emergency ward instead of the synagogue.

While on our way, we found a police officer on Renwick Avenue, a short distance from the place of injury. When he heard what had happened, he gave us good advice, "Get out of this neighborhood!" We did. The residents and nurses gave me wonderful treatment at the hospital, but Herta insisted that our good friend, Dr. Herbert Katz, an ophthalmologist (now retired in Florida), should also be called. We were very grateful that he was able to see me, too.

The police knew about the incident. Yet, my family kept the report out of the papers to avoid further friction between the black and white communities at the time. The day before, Dr. Kenneth Wright, a very well-liked specialist in geriatrics, had been similarly attacked while driving through the same section. Whenever I think of these incidents, or whenever I hear some black leaders make some most insensitive and unkind remarks about the Jews, I cannot help but get somewhat depressed. But, then I think of my black patients: Men, who have seen me for the first time shake my hand and say, "I was so glad to meet you, Sir." Black women of all ages kiss me on the cheek and tell me, "I prayed that you would be in today. I needed you." Thinking of that, it gives me hope again.

It was also in the sixties that I attended one of the yearly Medical Society meetings in New York City. Herta and I intended to go from there to Asbury Park by bus for a week's vacation. As we descended the escalator at the New York Port Authority bus terminal, my suitcase was on the step in front of me. A woman in back of me started a conversation, found out that I was a doctor, and asked for my card. "You never know if you might need a doctor in Syracuse," she said. A short while after, I picked up my little suitcase from the bottom of the stairway and heard the same woman scream for help. Some time later I was notified through her attorney that she had hurt her back severely after she had "fallen over" my suitcase. She asked for a large sum of money for her "damages." I discussed the case with attorneys Saul and Ed Alderman. Saul, Ed's father and the founder of the prestigious law firm, some years ago received the coveted Lawyer of the Year Award from the New York Bar Association. They set up an appointment for me for a pre-trial hearing in New York City. After my testimony, I was told by the attorney who handled my case in New York, "I think you did very well." I had only reported the truth, and I've heard nothing about the claim since. It was a real "nuisance case."

I am reminded of another incident in New York City. I had an appointment in the big city, and daughter Joan with husband Mel accompanied me on that trip. Mel parked his car on Central Park West. It was early Sunday afternoon, and we walked a few blocks to Eclair's, a European-style restaurant on 72nd Street. When we returned to the car about one hour later, we found that it had been skillfully unlocked and entered. The thieves had not bothered to open the trunk but were able to make a separation between the trunk and back seat. Aside from some of Joan's dresses and one of Mel's new suits, his Leica camera had been stolen. Only the Sunday *New York Times* lay untouched on the front seat. Fortunately, we thought, a police officer was standing at the corner, so Mel reported the theft to him. His answer was: "What else is new?"

As long as I am on the subject of disputes, I have to mention a case in which I was the claimant. One August day, I parked my car at Syracuse Upstate Medical Center's parking garage. When I was walking out of the garage, followed by Herta, I tripped and fell over the elevated curbstone. I suffered a rib fracture with atelectasis (collapsed lung). I went to see Dr. Fridtjof Nussbaumer, orthopedic specialist, who ordered the x-rays taken of me and sent me then to Dr. Martin Wynyard, a surgeon especially interested in thoracic diseases. Dr. Wynyard, who is half Jewish, also had to leave Nazi Germany. He went from Berlin to England and immigrated later to the United States. He mentioned to me that for years he had lost a lot of time from his surgical profession due to repeated upper respiratory infections, until he decided to follow the advice of the chemist and Nobel Prize winner Linus Pauling by taking very large doses of vitamin C. He treated me during my long disability period and was kind enough to testify as an expert medical witness in court for me. I asked our good friend, attorney Lawrence Bennett, to give me legal advice; Upstate Medical Center was represented by counselor James Gaul. As the case had to go before the State Court of Claims, Lawrence Bennett advised me to hire attorney Lewis Fineberg, a well-known trial lawyer, to represent me in court. My friend Rita Seligman accompanied us to the one-day hearing. There were witnesses from the lighting company, testimony about the weather, medical testimony by Dr. Wynyard, and both Herta and myself were questioned. A very nice judge was presiding, but there was no jury. I must have been very honest in all my answers, because even the opposing attorney mentioned that he would like to hire me as a doctor for the insurance companies he represents. (I can think of no duller job for a physician than to work for an insurance company. There is nothing better, for me at least, than the private practice of medicine.) This is what the Judge wrote in his decision:

> The Court was much impressed with Claimant, his demeanor and forthrightness and as a man of high moral standards and unquestionable integrity. However, the record supports the view that either the claimant was not watching where he was going or that he failed properly to negotiate the curb.

My claim was dismissed, but I learned first-hand about the judicial system's method of implementing reconciliation and atonement.

In-Laws

In 1966, my daughter Joan married Mel Raichelson, a graduate of the Syracuse University Department of Cultural Geography. He also took courses at the well-known Maxwell School of Public Administration where Theodore W. White and Daniel Moynihan were among his teachers. After his graduation, though, he went into banking, liked it, and stayed in that field.

One guest at the wedding was a man Herta had known in Breslau and met again while she was window shopping in Amsterdam, New York, in the 1940s. The man was Rabbi Kurt Metzger, who had been a student at the Jewish Theological Seminary in Breslau. Herta had taken care of the children of Israel Rabin, a professor at the Seminary, so she got to meet many of the students there. (Incidentally, one of the Rabin children in Herta's charge was Michael, who later became dean of Hebrew University in Jerusalem.) While living in Canajoharie, I'd let Dr. Metzger take the wheel of my car on some weekends; he had only a learner's permit while I'd had my hard-earned driver's license for almost a year. He headed Amsterdam's little synagogue then and now works in Monroe, New York. He is busy in prison work, and, as *Aufbau* reported, once got interested in a prisoner who had been falsely accused of murder and helped the man get his release. We were very pleased that he could attend Joan's wedding.

Reuben Raichelson, Mel's father, owned an electrical company. He had lost his wife (Mel's mother) years before to rheumatic heart disease and its complications. Mr. Raichelson was an avid sportsman and used to drive every weekend or so to the

Thousand Islands, where he kept a boat. In his last years he spent much of his time around Fort Lauderdale, Florida, and it was there that he suffered a very severe heart attack. After his return to Syracuse, his heart remained decompensated; he was fatigued and short of breath. He consulted Dr. Asher Black, a cardiologist, who ordered a heart catheterization at St. Joseph's Hospital. Dr. Black showed me the film of the coronary arteriogram. It was evident that the left heart ventricle was flabby and did not contract very well. A diagnosis of "aneurysm of the left ventricle" was made, and it was suggested that Dr. Donald Effler should perform open heart surgery. Mel's father discussed the proposed surgery with me, and I couldn't see any other alternative. Once a doctor, always a doctor.

There are two famous heart surgeons (and their staffs) in the city of Syracuse who serve a large population in the central New York area: Dr. Donald Effler at St. Joseph's Hospital and Dr. Fred Parker at the Upstate Medical Center. Dr. Effler had been chief of the Department of Thoracic and Cardiovascular Surgery at the Cleveland Clinic and is now chief cardiac surgeon at St. Joseph's Hospital in Syracuse. He founded the cardiac department here, after he left Cleveland in 1976 to avoid a forced retirement. One of his most famous patients was the late King Khaled of Saudi Arabia.

In the case of Mel's father, the doctor excised the aneurysm of his left heart ventricle. He was able for some time after surgery to drive up to the Thousand Islands. I definitely feel that it was imperative that Mel's father have the operation; yet after about three years, his heart gave out completely, and he died—unfortunately—at the age of 72.

Psychiatry

I attended a most enjoyable and memorable psychiatric seminar in the late 1960s, led by Dr. Ruth Burton, a clinical professor of psychiatry at Upstate Medical Center in Syracuse. She had practiced internal medicine for a number of years in Binghamton before deciding to go into psychiatry. After her arrival in Syracuse, she offered her course to all interested practitioners.

I remember well many of the people who attended her class. Some of the participants, like Dr. Max Marvin and Dr. William Schiffman, are now retired and live in Florida, while others, including Dr. Joseph Enders and Dr. Frank Meola, continue in private practice.

My late friend Dr. Hugo Stern, although in general practice, had always had a special interest in emotional diseases. He, like me, had escaped from Hitler Germany. Like me also, he was a fan of Siegmund Freud. How proud he was of a postcard he had received from Freud in answer to a question he had asked as a young doctor in Germany! Dr. Stern passed away at a relatively early age because of severe cardiac disease. He was especially interested in Dr. Burton's course, and, like all of us, hardly ever missed any of the weekly sessions. His widow Dina is a very well-known local portrait artist who has had many exhibitions in Syracuse.

Another of my classmates from Dr. Burton's course was Dr. Joseph Reidel, still actively practicing. About thirty years ago he became so famous that he made the headlines of the *New York Times,* his story made news overseas, and he was invited by

Secretary of State John Foster Dulles to a special cocktail party. The event that made him so famous took place in August 1955. He was sailing on a large sailboat on Lake Ontario with his wife and another doctor couple, when a heavy storm pounded the boat and threw Dr. Reidel overboard. He swam and swam for more than eight hours until almost midnight when he reached some heavy rocks. He rested there until daylight, when he was able to contact some strangers and the Coast Guard. He had been given up for dead by the Syracuse newspapers and by his own family but, at last, luckily, he was reunited with his loved ones.

Dr. Burton's course was very valuable. She pointed out that each one of us, just by practicing medicine, has had to use psychotherapy on every patient under our care. She told us the story of a young woman whose husband had left her, whose children were ill most of the time, who was in very poor financial circumstances, and who was depressed. "You would be crazy if you were not depressed," Dr. Burton had said to her, explaining that we often label things which might simply be normal reactions with psychiatric names. "Thank God for the compulsives," she used to remark, "for without them no work would be done."

I recall vividly that at one of our meetings Dr. Burton stated that a person who comes home from a day's work and, instead of joining friends for games and plays, goes to his room and reads a book is surely a schizophrenic. "Oh, my God," Dr. Reidel exclaimed in jest. "I must be a schizophrenic!" He was assured, though, that because of his job as a physician, seeing and interacting with patients all day, his case is certainly different. At the end of our course, which lasted about a year, Dr. Burton remarked: "I enjoyed every minute of it." And we all agreed.

One of the most interesting things we discussed in the course was an article written for the *New York Times Magazine* by Dr. Thomas Szasz, a professor of psychiatry at Syracuse's Upstate Medical Center. Sometimes called "America's most controversial psychiatrist," he has been invited to lecture in many major American cities, as well as many European countries and Japan. He has been on the Dick Cavett television show and in a debate with William F. Buckley. In this 1966 article, bearing the same name as his most often read book, *The Myth of Mental Illness,* he differentiated between voluntary and involuntary hospitalization, supporting only the former. Psychiatrists, in his opinion, are not really doctors but social engineers. There is no "mental illness"; therefore no one can speak of "treatment" of a patient committed to a mental hospital. As a matter of fact, Doctor Szasz calls the physician who commits a patient a "jailer." None of our small physician group in Dr. Burton's class was able to see eye to eye with Dr. Szasz. Years later, at a medical convention in Hawaii, I asked one of the psychiatrists who attended what he thought of Dr. Szasz's ideas. "I don't have to tell you," he replied, "that I don't agree with them." And another psychiatrist practicing in Syracuse told me, "You know that he is wrong. It is an untrue denial. There is mental illness." American psychiatric opinion with regard to *The Myth of Mental Illness* is best summarized in Alfred M. Freedman's *Modern Synopsis of Psychiatry,* "While some of Szasz's ideas have probably led to a useful reexamination of requirements for mental hospitalization . . . many question the often negative effect of his thinking on the public's attitude toward psychiatry."

There have been many other areas of disagreement between the Syracuse professor and the majority of psychiatrists. He is the author of a book called *Schizophrenia* which tries to prove that there is no such disease. In spite of his books, all psychiatric textbooks and medical journals continue to use the word and to discuss the treatment of the illness; apparently, their authors were not too much impressed by Szasz. They were also not impressed by the doctor's stand that suicidal psychotics should never be involuntarily hospitalized. Szasz is convinced that neither the state and federal governments, nor psychiatrists, have any right to interfere with a person's intention to kill himself. One of the most riticized articles by Dr. Szasz appeared in a 1975 edition of *Medical Economics.* "Stop poking around in your patients' lives!" he said, advising the nonpsychiatric physician to avoid giving advice to the patient on "non-physical" matters. In contrast, I remember a lecture at a general session of the A.M.A. given by Dr. Gene

Usdin, clinical professor of psychiatry at Louisiana State University and author of *Psychiatry in General Medical Practice*. He told us that, for all they know about their patients, some psychiatrists could just as well be veterinarians (without denying that veterinarians have a lot of compassion), while many general medical practitioners, just by their intuition and interest in the patient, can bring about a patient's emotional recovery.

Aside from *The Myth of Mental Illness, Schizophrenia,* and numerous articles and book reviews, Dr. Szasz also wrote the following books: *Law, Liberty and Psychiatry; The Manufacture of Madness; Psychiatric Justice; Ethics of Psychoanalysis; The Myth of Psychotherapy; The Theology of Medicine; Sex by Prescription;* and *Karl Kraus and the Souldoctors*. All these books are well written, learned, and fun to read. The drawback is that very few psychiatrists or primary physicians agree with the doctor's conclusions. More recently, two books were published by Prometheus Books: *Thomas Szasz: Primary Values and Major Contentions,* edited by Richard E. Vatz and Lee S. Weinberg, and *The Therapeutic State,* a collection of his magazine articles and book reviews.

I received a special benefit from the doctor's writings in an indirect way. In May of 1979 I read an article by Dr. Ronald Pies, chief psychiatric resident at Syracuse's Upstate Medical Center. The title was "On Myths and Counter Myths: More on Szaszian Fallacies." When I asked the young physician for a reprint, he sent along with the photostat a little note expressing his interest in my own work. When I answered that I was only a general practitioner, he referred me to an article by Dr. Daniel Freedman in the *A.M.A. Journal* that said that about 60 percent of mental diseases are diagnosed and treated by general physicians. Later, I saw pieces by Dr. Pies in the *A.M.A. News* and in the *New York Times Magazine,* and I found the above-mentioned article, originally published in the *Archives of General Psychiatry,* reprinted in the book about Szasz recently issued by Prometheus. While assistant professor of psychology and coordinator of emergency mental health at Pennsylvania State University, Pies wrote a most helpful book: *Inside Psychotherapy: The Patient's Handbook.* In

February of 1984 he spoke before the Central New York branch of the American Psychiatric Association. I got a special invitation to this talk through the Association's very active secretary, Ms. Peggy Flanders, and was able to meet him in person. We are in constant touch now. He has moved to a new position in Boston. I know he will go places. Aside from his professional interest in writing on psychiatry, he has also written some short stories and poetry.

Heritage: Jews and Christian Heaven

It was 1973 when our Onondaga County Medical Society, in conjunction with the Medical Society of the State of New York, sponsored a teaching trip to Hawaii. The whole package was fairly inexpensive, and my son-in-law Mel, a mortgage representative, asked me how I could afford *not* to go. So, I went. The trip only lasted for a little over a week, but Herta was unfortunately suffering from a herniated disk in her back and was not able to join me. She had been examined in consultation by Dr. Stephen Bastable, the orthopedic specialist, and Dr. Herbert Lourie, the neurosurgeon, some time before. No surgery was considered.

    I looked forward to meeting Dr. Stanley Batkin in Honolulu, where he was teaching neurophysiology. Dr. Batkin had practiced in Syracuse and had examined my son Michael for neurological consultation there. Dr. Stanley Leslie, a Syracuse gynecologist, had also wanted to see him but was unable to make it. I met Dr. Batkin at the University of Hawaii with Dr. Joseph Lukaszewicz, a family practitioner, and after lunch we went to a Japanese tea garden. We reminisced about Syracuse, of course, and spoke about the chances Dr. Lukaszewicz's son would have of graduating from Hawaii's Medical College in the future. Unfortunately, that college in Honolulu had still to be completed, and all the Hawaiian students had to go to the mainland to finish their medical studies. As I mentioned, only those students who get the highest marks on certain tests and in particular subjects have a chance to be admitted to American medical colleges; it is not always the best selection process. Many prominent physicians face the same problem with the children who want to follow in their footsteps. Luckily, Dr. Lukaszewicz's son graduated from a medical school in Mexico, took his internship and residency in this country, and has just recently taken over his father's practice after his father's retirement to Florida. He will do just fine. To the best of my knowledge, the young Dr. L. speaks at three languages: English, as he grew up in these United States; Polish, the native language of his parents; and Spanish, since he had his medical education in Mexico.

I found Hawaii to be a most friendly place. When we arrived at Honolulu Airport, we were covered with flowers and showered with kisses by beautiful hula-girls and taken by bus to our hotel—the Hawaiian Regent. It was late Friday afternoon, and we still had to register, but I decided to try to attend Friday night Sabbath services at the Reform Temple Emanuel. It was late, and the temple was pretty far away, but the taxi driver at the hotel assured me that he would get me there in time. He also suggested that I call him after the services, and he would get me back to my hotel.

The services were led by Rabbi Julius Nodel, formerly of St. Louis, who gave a sermon about the Jews and Jesus. The service was conducted partly in English, and partly—as is the case all over the world—in Hebrew. Before it ended, I was questioning the wisdom of calling my taxi driver, knowing the long distance between Temple Emanuel and my hotel, so I asked three ladies who were sitting in my row if they could drop me off downtown. They promised that they would. After the service, the rabbi asked us to stay for the *Oneg Schabbath,* a Friday night party at which friends and strangers commonly meet for a cup of coffee and some cookies. When the three ladies did not follow me, I asked them whether they intended to participate in the *Oneg Schabbath.*

"No," one answered, "but, if you wish to, we shall wait for you."

Then it dawned me, and I asked, "Are you Jewish at all?"

"No," the women replied. "But do you hold against us what happened in Germany?"

"Of course not," I answered. We rode to the hotel together.

They were three good women, apparently in the real estate business together, and they belonged to a Christian fundamentalist church. They had attended the services because they had seen an ad in the newspaper about the sermon on Jews and Jesus saying that everybody was welcome at Temple Emanuel. They were happy, they said, that the Lord had sent me to them that Friday evening. Naturally, I felt very proud that they considered me such an important person, especially since I had been thrown out of Germany about thirty-five years before as a member of an "inferior race." I praised the ladies for their courage in giving me, a stranger, a lift from far away Pali Highway to downtown Honolulu. "You don't look too dangerous to us," one of the women replied.

Soon they placed on my seat a pamphlet written by Shira Lindsay, a "Jewish believer," about Messianic Judaism. Shortly after my return to Syracuse, I found a report on Shira Lindsay in *Time* magazine: Daughter of a Dallas pentecostal evangelist, she had converted to Judaism in Boston and then moved to Israel in 1970. After her arrival, she tried to spread the Gospel among the Jews, and the rabbis in Boston annulled her conversion to Judaism.

The ride went quickly, and I was dropped off at my hotel. It was strange. I had not been away very long, but the lobby certainly looked different. I went upstairs to my hotel room and tried to open my room door with my key, but I did not succeed. The guard came upstairs to help me, but he also was not successful. "Are you sure you are at the right hotel?" he finally asked. Instead of the Hawaiian Regent, the ladies had dropped me off at the neighboring Holiday Inn. I did not hold it against them, of course.

I phoned them before my departure from Hawaii and thanked them by letter after my return to Syracuse. I mentioned that I had a little cold and received by airmail some beautiful cut flowers and a note inscribed, "To Dr. Hartmann from his Christian friends." This was followed by a gift from one of the women of the Old Testament Prophecy Edition of the New Testament, with these words written on the inside page: "Dr. Hartmann, sharing with you my most priceless possession." She did not realize, of course, that I had at least three other copies of the same edition sent to me by Christian friends. Each one of the ladies sent me a letter, and I answered each in turn. "You love the Jews so much," I wrote to one of them. "Don't you see that they would disappear if you converted them all?"

"They would not disappear," the third one retorted. "They would remain Jews, as 'complete Jews.'"

In my final letter I expressed my view that one had to be either a Jew or a Christian, that there is nothing in between. I am grateful to my Hawaiian correspondents because they forced me to think my position through and to make it clearer to myself and others.

You cannot get away from your heritage. A few years ago, we Syracuse physicians were invited by one of the larger local factories for a tour and a discussion of the health care of their employees. Following the discussion I was seated at a dinner table with two Jewish colleagues: Dr. Baurice Laffer, former Syracuse police physician, and Dr. Jesse Serby, another family practitioner. We were joined by Dr. Reskallah, a gynecologist, whom we had never met before but whom I had heard about on the television show "Jewish Journal." Dr. Ernest Sarason, who had been honored by the Medical Society for his fundraising efforts for Jewish and general causes, was the guest on the show. He spoke about his trip to Egypt, and he mentioned that Dr. Reskallah had given him the names and addresses of some important Cairo physicians whom he was able to meet. At our dinner, Dr. Reskallah told us that he was a Coptic Christian and had read the Bible several times. He graduated from Cairo University many, many years ago, and said that he was at a loss to understand that some Jews don't seem interested in their Jewish heritage. He, himself, felt that he was a "completed Jew." Here he fell into the trap of the so-called Hebrew or Jewish Christians. You are either a Jew or a Christian, not both. The last time I met Dr. Reskallah, he was retiring from active practice to join the Army Medical Corps.

You cannot get away from your heritage. The shocking result of a too rigid orthodox religious teaching was shown to me in the attitude of some German women domestics who asked their Jewish employer, "Don't you fee bad, Mrs. ——, that the Jews killed Jesus?" That seemed to be all they remembered from their religious instruction.

On a "Phil Donahue Show" about politics and religion, the host asked a young fundamentalist Christian girl whether she thought that a Jew who led an exemplary life could expect to get to Heaven. The girl, visibly embarrassed, hemmed and hawed but finally blurted out that the Jew would have to go to Hell. The Bible told her so. She saw no discrepancy between a loving religion and such a harsh God.

Mr. Donahue then ran a clip from a previous show on which he had asked the Reverend Jerry Falwell of the Moral Majority the same question. The Reverend seemed evasive at first, but then he pointed to a Jewish friend of his in the audience whose name he even mentioned. He did not go so far as to say that his Jewish friend would go to Hell, but he felt that his friend could not get to Heaven unless he was converted. For Reverend Falwell, this idea extends as well to secularists and humanists, even if they are of high moral fiber.

Merrill Simon, an Orthodox Jewish writer, wrote sympathetically about the Reverend in his book *Jerry Falwell and the Jews*. Mr. Simon, like some Jews in the States and Israel, believes that because of the fundamentalist minister's friendship with Israel, one can support him in all his views. But the majority of Jews cannot agree with a gentleman who looks upon Judaism as an inferior religion that should be replaced by his particular fundamentalist brand of Christianity. We remember well from our childhood study of Jewish Scriptures: "The righteous of all faiths will have their share in the world to come."

But, the Moral Majority leader showed his objection to that idea again when he appeared as a panelist on a television show about Armageddon, moderated by Sandy Freeman. A woman caller, who had come from Israel, hinted that people in that country could not identify with Reverend Falwell and his belief that his brand of religion, in contrast to Judaism, Islam, and even other Christian religions, was the only right one. Mr. Falwell explained that this woman did not understand his views and therefore did not tell the truth.

"But, Reverend Falwell," Sandy Freeman interrupted, "didn't you tell me—at least twice on this show—that Jews cannot go to Heaven?"

Mr. Falwell did not give a direct answer. Instead, he turned to Reverend Jim Wallis, another panelist on the show, and asked if Wallis did not hold the same views as he did in regard to Jews who do not believe in Christ. Reverend Wallis seemed a little startled at first, as Ms. Freeman and the caller had not directed their questions to him, but the evangelist answered that he would not dare to make a decision about the fate of the non-believer—he would leave the judgment up to God.

Too bad that everyone is not so accepting: A few days later, on the television show "Crossfire," the guest was Reverend Jimmy Swaggart, a most successful television evangelist. He was asked about his ideas on salvation for Jews, Catholics, or other Protestants. Mr. Swaggart said that he couldn't promise salvation to anyone but himself. The Bible told him so.

In the 1980 Religious Roundtable national affairs briefing in Dallas, Reverend Bailey Smith, a fundamentalist Christian minister and president of the Southern Baptist Convention, stated, "God almighty does not hear the prayer of a Jew." This remark caused a big commotion among Jews and non-Jews, and the pastor did eventually discuss the insensitivity of his comment with Jewish leaders in the United States and Israel.

Yet, you cannot blame these moral, decent, even "philosemitic" gentlemen for their views, which are in complete accordance with their literal understanding of the Bible.

They don't see that the Bible is, in reality, a book of mercy and compassion that shows a great deal of humor in dealing with people of many nations and beliefs. In Dr. Martin Grotjahn's book *Beyond Laughter,* the noted psychoanalyst retells the witty story of Balak, king of Moab, who hired the prophet Balaam to curse the people of Israel. But, the story goes, the Lord did not like that and put all kinds of obstructions in the prophet's way. In the end, Balaam was forced to bless the Jewish people instead.

The king of Moab was quite angry and took the prophet from one place to another to bring about a curse, but Balaam's blessings came louder and clearer.

This sense of humor, so sorely missing from the teachings of the fundamentalists, is most essential in overcoming our human difficulties. Surely it is important not to take oneself too seriously and to find something to smile about even in the most hurtful situations. Everybody has probably seen opera singer Beverly Sills in one of her many guest appearances on television talk shows. She always delights her audience not only with her songs, but also with her charming stories. Born of Jewish parents, married to an Episcopalian, she became the mother of a severely retarded son and a deaf daughter. Once, quite discouraged, she said to her mother, Mrs. Silverman, "Isn't it terrible that Muffy cannot hear?" Her mother's reply was, "Aren't you glad that she doesn't need any glasses?"

In October 1963 Herta and I were returning from a visit to our relatives in California, and we traveled by train, as I still suffer from motion sickness on plane rides. In the dining car we happened to meet an elderly poet from Nebraska named William J. Shallcross and a congenial young nun from Ohio. We all exchanged letters for a short time, and the meeting must have impressed me enough to compose the following poem:

> Returning East on the crowded train,
> The Central New York ride was not in vain;
> We met a poet, we met a nun,
> And we had certainly lots of fun.
> The poet said to the nun in her robe—
> While discussing the merits of John, the late Pope—
> That he, although being a Protestant,
> Had worked with Catholics hand in hand;
> And he found this meeting an occasion,
> To stress again his admiration.
> The nun, she answered with a smile so big:
> "Then you know, that I am a Catholic?"
> She also declared in that train-dining-hall,
> That, wearing her robe, was no hardship at all.

> In contrast to other girls, she has never to guess,
> What hat she should wear or what kind of a dress.
> We Jews at the table found here proof to the rumor,
> That true religion shows a keen sense of humor.
> And somehow we saw some hopeful rays
> Of understanding in future days.
> The reader should not consider a crime,
> That some of my sentences do not rhyme.
> I am not a poet, as you can see,
> But just an ordinary M.D.
> Best wishes to Buddhists, Christians, and Jews.
> To all, from Heinz Hartmann in Syracuse.

Unfortunately, the lack of humor and the harsh judgment of people with other beliefs by the Fundamentalists stands in the way of universal brotherhood. Keep in mind that Reverend Falwell cannot be invited as a speaker to our Syracuse Area Interreligious Council because of his lack of tolerance for our members with their various denominations.

Compare this to the attitude of Father Andrew F. Morlion, Chancellor of the International University of Social Studies *Pro Deo* in Rome. He was invited by Dr. Arthur Sackler, an international publisher who considers himself a humanist-scientist, to write an article about the non-believer and faith for the *Medical Tribune*. Let me quote Father Morlion: "The non-believer who rejects selfishness for altruism is religious, even without knowing it. We can conclude that, in equally loving ways, God is always near to and actively present in all persons of good will."

Dr. Sackler was surprised that the eminent Catholic clergyman invited him to be the international chairman of the American Pro Deo Council, and he admitted that he is not a religious man. "I acknowledge my heritage. I practice no rituals. I accept no dogmas," Sackler wrote. In a beautiful reply in *Medical Tribune's* pages, Father Morlion concluded:

> Are you a man of faith? The answer is not to be found by checking dogmas, concepts, and the ideas that we profess. To

find the answer we must examine our own lives. Have I lived and served all of my fellow men, even and especially those who neither love nor serve me? If the answer is yes, then you are indeed a man of faith.

Not a day goes by that I am not reminded of my heritage. People tell me that I should forget what happened so many years ago. I cannot, nor do I want to.

Frustrations

I have always found the practice of medicine to be very rewarding, but it is not without its frustrations. Recently, the various medical boards have come out with new regulations requiring every physician to apply for a Physician's Recognition Award by attending a certain number of courses or lectures. I used to attend American Medical Association meetings in New York and elsewhere, and I had to sign my name in a book at the end of the program. The secretaries in charge of the attendance book got so high-and-mighty after a while that they would not let a doctor sign if he left the meeting a few minutes before the end. I've gotten a little tired of this, so several years ago, I resumed attending the medical Grand Rounds on Thursday mornings at Upstate Medical Center. The speakers are local professors or guest lecturers from medical centers all over the country. The chairman is Dr. William J. Williams, professor of medicine and chief of the medical department.

Things like these requirements for the Physicians' Recognition Award and higher and higher malpractice insurance rates take some of the pleasure out of practicing medicine. As far as regulations for course attendance are concerned, it is my firm conviction that the average doctor can be trusted to keep up with new developments, without the force of law.

Another problem taking some satisfaction away from the practice of medicine is the drug habit of so many younger and older people. For me, personally, alcohol and nicotine addiction have never been problems. In my medical practice, though, I have to deal with these tragic situations extensively. (Alcoholics Anonymous and similar organizations have been most helpful, but it is important to put the alcoholic person on mild tranquilizers during withdrawal periods.) Some patients try to sell the drugs on the black market, others collect prescriptions from several doctors and take an overdose. But, despite the misuse of some controlled substances by a number of patients, it would be irresponsible to completely withhold narcotics or tranquilizers from patients in severe pain or in emotional turmoil.

Getting patients to quit smoking is never an easy task. Most readily admit that nicotine abuse might cause lung cancer or cardiovascular complications. They still take a chance or claim that the cigarettes might help them lose weight by suppressing their appetite. Hypnosis has helped some people kick the habit; a new chewing gum medication, developed by the Merrell-Dow Company, has helped others. To be helped, the chainsmoker has to be serious about leaving his habit. Friends of mine who conquered their cigarette addictions switched to the pipe. Their reason? They don't inhale, they say. They do. But, even if they didn't, we, the nonsmokers, would get all the smoke, and many of us who are exposed to it have conjunctivitis reactions, requiring us to use eyedrops several times a day. Besides, the pipe smoker risks being afflicted with at least cancer of the lip or mouth.

One cannot prevent obesity by smoking cigarettes. Regular exercise will help a little. In winter time or bad weather, I (for example) use an exercycle. I recall an article written years ago by Dr. Irvine Page, editor emeritus of *Modern Medicine*. He told us that while pedaling, one can read the medical journals. Good advice.

I don't prescribe certain controlled substances anymore—heavy sleep preparations, for example, or the amphetamines. I still use other medications for weight control, as I know that without this "crutch" the majority of patients are unable to follow a reducing diet. It goes without saying that the treatment of obesity is a must for people with severe cardiac disease, hypertension, and many diabetic conditions. I feel that the prescription of an appetite suppressant is preferable to wiring of the jaw or an intestinal bypass operation.

There was a medical lecture by the Academy for Family Physicians at Syracuse's Northway Inn. The topic was "hypertension," and the speaker was Dr. Robert Scheer, one of the leading nephrologists here, while another leading nephrologist, Dr. Bernard Bernstein, and a professor of endocrinology, Dr. David Streeten, participated in the lively discussion. I happened to raise the question about the role of obesity in high blood pressure. It was the general consensus that obesity itself has very little to do with hypertension; it is the fluid retention in overweight patients that is responsible for the rise in blood pressure. Yet, soon afterward, I read reports from Israel and the United States which showed that one group of patients with hypertension was treated for their obesity only, while the other group received diuretics or water pills. The group treated for obesity lowered their pressure as much, if not more, than the diuretic-treated group. If the obese patient loses weight, blood pressure comes down and stays down without further need of antihypertensive medication.

Not only for weight control, but also for constipation, diabetic conditions, and the prevention of arteriosclerotic heart disease and colon cancer, the high fiber diet has been recommended for the past decade. First described by Drs. Burkitt, Walker, and Painter in an article published in the *Journal of the American Medical Association,* the "Save Your Life Diet" was popularized by Dr. David Reuben. He is, of course, the author of *Everything You Always Wanted to Know about Sex but Were Afraid to Ask.*

What about my health and the health of my family? Herta has a weight problem, aggravating her herniated disk disease and causing a diabetic condition. But she is very happy to have Joan and Mel living next door with our grandchildren Sarah and Maurice. Sarah is 14 as of this writing, and Maurice is 12. Sarah is very proud to take care of our 15-year-old dog Rusty; we also share three cats between us: Rocky, Robin, and Raquel. The children are in good health, and so is Joan. Mel also is generally in good health, but he suffered a severe gall bladder attack three years ago while we were at the Concord in the Catskills. I tried to relieve his pain there as well as I could and had him examined in

Syracuse by Dr. Hans Bruns, renowned gastroenterologist, who referred him to Dr. Ernest Sarason for surgery.

In general, my health has been pretty good, except for the emotional scars I was left with from my terrible Nazi past in Germany. During my first years in Syracuse, I had an occasional medical check-up by Dr. Max Kutzer or Dr. Fred Hiss, internists and cardiologists, both of whom I had asked for consultations in my private practice. They both were located in the State Tower Building, where I am now—the finest building I have ever occupied. When Dr. Hiss—now age 90—retired about twenty-five years ago, I already knew that I had developed high blood pressure, hypertension. No physician should treat himself. "There is an old German proverb," I said to Mel, "A doctor who treats himself has a fool for a patient." (Whenever I tell him a new "old German proverb," he says, "Again?" He probably has heard too many of them. "How come," he asked me on the fortieth anniversary of my arrival in the United States, "you have been here for more years than I am old, and you still talk with such an accent?") Anyway, Dr. Murray Grossman, professor of medicine at Upstate Medical Center, has advised me medically for the past twenty-five years. Drs. Harold Smulyan and David Nash took care of me a few times while Dr. Grossman was on a sabbatical year in Utah. More recently, Dr. Paul Kronenberg, also a professor at Upstate, helped me out during Dr. Grossman's absence.

Because of my hypertension, I began taking on renese, a potent diuretic. I was also instructed to drink orange juice and eat bananas and other fruits rich in potassium to prevent the loss of this important metal through excretion. In spite of all this, my potassium serum level always stayed low, and there were also electrocardiographic changes, typical for potassium depletion, although my blood pressure returned to normal. Dr. Grossman then advised me to take some extra medication, like K Lyte and K Lor, but to no avail. We switched to a potassium sparing agent, a drug called diazyde, and my potassium level has remained normal since. But, then Dr. Grossman found some arrhythmia and advised me to switch from regular to decaffeinated coffee. At that time I felt that I needed the energy "real" coffee gives and asked to be allowed to drink at least two or three cups a day. On a later visit to my doctor's office, the electrocardiogram showed a more pronounced arrhythmia, a greater number of P.V.C.s (premature ventricular contractions). These arrhythmias, as a rule, are not treated unless an underlying heart condition exists. We came to an agreement, though, that it would not hurt to try to regulate my heartbeat. I was put on atenolol (tenormin), and my pulse and heartbeat have become regular. I also switched completely to decaffeinated coffee. This switch did not make me feel any more tired, but it helped me in some other, unrelated situation. Since childhood I had fasted from sundown to sundown on the Day of Atonement. For many years I suffered a most severe headache that started hours before the end of Yom Kippur. Since I discontinued drinking regular coffee, these headaches have not returned, and I have come to the definite conclusion that they had represented withdrawal symptoms—caused by the withdrawal of caffeine. Now that my organism is not used to this stimulant anymore, I do not miss my coffee on the fast day. I have been reading similar findings in case reports in the medical literature.

It has been easier to take care of Michael since we moved from our home office on South Salina Street to Syracuse's suburb of DeWitt. (Living in the country, but still close to the city, our neighbors consist of black and white people, Jews and Gentiles, natives of the United States as well as immigrants of Chinese, Indian, and Lebanese descent.) In addition to his retardation and seizures, Michael suffers from allergies all through the year. I learned again from him how important psychosomatic medicine and communication are. One day his eyes looked especially red and irritated, and our good friend Briggi exclaimed, "The poor boy. Look at his eyes." He probably felt sorry for himself, and he started to scream. The next day he was seen by Dr. Herbert Katz, the ophthalmologist, who said to Eleene, "He looks like a million dollars." Michael beamed.

The physician's interest, of course, does not limit itself to the ailments of his own family, or to plain physical ailments, or to his own private patients. Even if he is retired or semi-retired, the physician's interest does not diminish. Several years ago I heard

Mrs. Sue Wilson of Syracuse speak in the Adult Education Series at Temple Society of Concord. She talked about the Moonies, as she had lost a son to the Unification Church. I had never met her before, but after her lecture I phoned her a few times about the problem. She unfortunately passed away at a young age after a long illness. I often think of our dentist friend whose illness was diagnosed as Alzheimer's disease. Although the treatment still leaves much to be desired, we share with his family the hope that eventually this elusive ailment will also be conquered. As the saying goes, "Once a doctor, always a doctor."

Judaic Studies

Taking care of health problems is a most important part of my life, but medical practice alone—even though it brings me face to face with birth, life, and death—does not do enough to help me define my place in life. For that, I have continually turned to the study of my Jewish heritage.

In the early 1970s, I spent many years on the steering committee for the adult education series of the Jewish Community Center in Syracuse. The committee was chaired by Mrs. Ida Benderson, who was most active not only in the Jewish Community Center, but also in general civic affairs of the city. In recognition, Syracuse's mayor named the Ida Benderson Senior Citizen Center after her. The adult education series was held once every year. The classes began with one or two keynote speakers of national prominence and continued with a Jewish study course that lasted about six weeks. Gradually, more and more Jewish study courses were made available to the public through the local synagogues, and lectures by well-known Jewish speakers about Jewish themes were sponsored in great numbers, so that by the later 1970s the adult education series became unnecessary.

After my activities with the adult education series had ended, I completed a correspondence course on Basic Studies in Judaism and Christianity, for which I received a certificate by The Academy For Jewish Studies Without Walls in New York.

At the 1977 annual meeting of the Onondaga County Society, I heard the inaugural address of Dr. David Poushter, professor for ear, nose, and throat diseases. He has been active in general and Jewish causes and is much valued as a consultant in his specialty. He talked about the history of medicine and—because of his Jewish heritage—quoted from the Bible as well as from Maimonides, one of his favorite physicians, who lived in the twelfth century.

I had always been interested in the field of Jews and medicine, and in March 1978 I gave a talk in Temple Concord's adult education series entitled "Judaism, Jews, Medicine, and Medical Ethics." I was introduced by Mrs. Joan Silverman, chairwoman of the lecture series, and I was happy to see in the audience some of the Jewish medical students from Upstate Medical College. They had been specially invited by Dr. Harry Feldman, professor of preventive medicine, who was always interested in the education of these young medical men. Dr. Feldman is widely known because of his work on toxoplasmosis, and he, together with Dr. Albert Sabin, developed a test for the diagnosis of this disease.

After my talk I was encouraged to publish that speech in one of our medical magazines. I thought of Dr. Michael Halberstam (brother of Pulitzer Prize winner David Halberstam) who was editor of *Modern Medicine* at that time. He also is the author of *A Coronary Event* and the novel *The Wanting of Levine,* a professor of medicine, a heart specialist, and was known to me for years for his numerous, well-written articles in the *New York Times Magazine* and other publications. I sent the manuscript to Dr. Halberstam and was surprised to receive a fairly long letter from him. I was tickled that he had taken the time to read it and to go over it with me in detail. "Thank you very much for sending me your excellent manuscript," he wrote. "I found it fascinating on several levels, but regret that in its present form it is not suitable for use in *Modern Medicine.*" He continued to explain that while my complete article, with its historical and ethical implications, is of interest to the editors, the general medical magazine reader might prefer more direct and practical articles. In my reply, I thanked Dr. Halberstam for his kind interest, but I, as a "generalist," felt unable to change my paper and to divide it into several smaller, focused pieces. I intended to shelve my manuscript and possibly offer it to one of the larger Jewish periodicals later.

About two years later I was saddened and shocked to read in the headlines of all the major papers and all the medical journals that Dr. Halberstam had been shot and killed by a "millionaire burglar." (Apparently the man had amassed a fortune by breaking into wealthy people's homes.) Late one night, returning to his Washington, D.C. home with his wife, the doctor was mortally wounded by two bullets in his chest. Still, he tried to drive to a nearby hospital. On the way, the physician noticed the fleeing intruder and swerved his car into the man, who was later arrested by police. Unfortunately, Dr. Halberstam had lost so much blood that he died on the operating table. He was 49 years old. So many beautiful obituaries were written, including one by Dr. Irving H. Page, learned editor emeritus of *Modern Medicine,* who had originally recommended Michael Halberstam to be his successor. Time has passed, but it is still impossible to understand such a senseless crime. An annual Michael J. Halberstam Lecture at George Washington University in Washington, D.C. has been established in his memory by *Modern Medicine.*

After learning of this absurd tragedy, the publication of my talk about Judaism, Jews, Medicine, and Medical Ethics didn't seem so urgent anymore. I had sent the manuscript to a few Jewish periodicals though. Some of the Jewish magazines didn't really have the space for my lengthy article, and one of them folded. Finally, I thought of Trude Weiss Rosmarin, editor of the independent *Jewish Spectator,* whom Rabbi Robert Gordis, the widely known scholar, called "the most Jewishly learned woman in the world." I sent her the manuscript and was pleased to hear that the *Spectator* was eager to publish it—except for some revisions I would have to make. Aside from the necessity of eliminating names and facts of local Syracuse interest, I would have to give more dates and sources to give the paper a more scientific look. I revised the lecture and made some additions, but it was not enough.

Ms. Weiss Rosmarin replied, from her editorial offices in Los Angeles, that my revisions would have to go further, that all references to Jewish sources should be precisely checked. I felt that I really would have to be able to read the Bible and the

Talmud in their original language, instead of depending on secondary translations, to satisfy the scholarly editor and readership of the *Jewish Spectator*. With my continued active practice and other projects in mind, I declined to make any further revisions, but I thanked the lady for her continued admirable editorials and book reviews which have been and are still of great help to me.

Interestingly enough, though, I found Trude Weiss Rosmarin's name a short time later, when I was skimming through the pages of Ernest Jones's biography of Freud. Jones discusses one of Freud's last books, *Moses and Monotheism*, and its claim that Moses was an Egyptian. Many Jewish Bible-experts disagreed with Freud, including T. W. Rosmarin who published a little booklet: *The Hebrew Moses: An Answer to Siegmund Freud*. She criticized Freud for writing in a field "reserved for specialist scholars." She also stated that nobody should do research on biblical topics if he has not mastered Hebrew, Egyptian, and "many other neighboring languages of the Near East as well." Jones found her criticisms most unfair and took Mrs. Rosmarin sharply to task for them.

I recently ran into Mrs. Rosmarin's name again when I reviewed the third volume of Maurice Friedman's *Martin Buber's Life and Work* for the *Jewish Observer* in Syracuse. In 1953, Professor Buber accepted the Peace Prize of the German Book Trade at St. Paul's Church in Frankfurt. The editor of the *Jewish Spectator* wrote an article attacking Buber because he had given his speech in a church. The professor's comment was, "I am somewhat astonished at Trude Rosmarin. The Paulskirche has very long ago ceased to be a church; it is a kind of universalist and democratic symbol." He added that the two other Peace Prizes, to Schweitzer and Guardini, had also been given at St. Paul's Church, "so it is a kind of tradition."

On October 15, 1979, a symposium was held at the Temple Society of Concord, under the title "Judaism in Christian Theology and Preaching." One of the best of its kind anywhere, the meeting was sponsored by the Syracuse Area Interreligious Council, Hendricks Chapel, and the B. G. Rudolph Lectures in

Judaic Studies of Syracuse University. Most helpful for the arrangement of the symposium were Professor Leland Jamison, director of the Rudolph Lectures, Mrs. Dorothy Rose, executive director of the Syracuse Area Interreligious Council, and Professor Alan Berger, chairman of the Jewish Studies Program at Syracuse University. Rabbi Theodore Levy was and is Senior Rabbi of Temple Concord, where the symposium was held. The meeting was moderated by Professor Darrell Fashing, then assistant dean of Hendricks Chapel and now a professor of religion in Florida.

The one-day symposium was held on a weekday, and I was not on vacation. When I saw the topic and the list of speakers, I just knew I had to attend. A doctor friend covered for me, I notified my answering service, and I put a note on my office door saying that I was attending a meeting. The symposium was well attended, but somehow the camera crew of CBS got several closeup pictures of me, which were shown on noon-time television, so that my family and a number of patients realized what "meeting" I had been to.

It was such a wonderful symposium that I shall mention the names of the illustrious speakers, all scholars of worldwide reputation. There was Paul Van Buren, Protestant theologian and professor of religion at Temple University; Dr. Eugene Fischer, executive director of the Office of Catholic-Jewish Relations for the National Conference of Catholic Bishops; Dr. Krister Stendahl, professor at Harvard Divinity School—a Lutheran—who only recently has been named Bishop of Stockholm in the Church of Sweden; and Dr. Michael Cook, professor of intertestamental and early Christian literature at Hebrew Union College, who accepted the invitation to participate in the symposium on rather short notice because of Dr. Samuel Sandmel's serious illness. A friend, colleague, and former student, Dr. Cook had been highly recommended by Professor Sandmel.

Unfortunately, a short time after the symposium, Dr. Sandmel passed away. I had heard him speak in Syracuse on several occasions. He was as well versed in New Testament Studies as any Christian scholar, and he was recognized for his activity in Jewish-Christian relations. He headed the team of twenty-nine scholars who edited the New English Bible in 1976. I was irked quite a few years ago when I leafed through the 16-volume *Encyclopedia Judaica* and was unable to find Samuel Sandmel's name anywhere. I contacted the Jerusalem editor and was assured that an article about this great scholar would appear in the forthcoming yearbook. I realized, of course, that the inclusion of Dr. Sandmel in the *Encyclopedia Judaica* was not of the utmost importance to him. I wrote him, though, and received the following reply on March 21, 1975:

Dear Dr. Hartmann:
      Thank you for your kind letter and thank you for your kindness. I have been unaware of not being listed in the *Encyclopedia Judaica* until I read a review of the *Encyclopedia* in a British journal, which scolded the editors for what was described as an excessive Israeli preoccupation and a relative neglect of the rest of the world. In one section he mentioned unmentioned people and included me in that list! Thank you very much. All good wishes.
                                        Cordially,
                                        Samuel Sandmel

It took many years until my little article about Samuel Sandmel finally appeared in the 1982 *Decennial Book* of the *Encyclopedia Judaica*. I sent a photostat of my small biographical essay and an explanatory letter to his secretary of many years, Mrs. Sam November, who, in turn, forwarded the material to his widow, Frances Fox Sandmel. I was very pleased to receive a beautiful letter from Mrs. Sandmel, who graciously expressed her appreciation for the short writeup I did.

The book reporting on our symposium, edited by Dr. Darrell Fashing, was published by the Edwin Mellen Press about a year ago. The volume is dedicated to the memory of Dr. Samuel Sandmel. In addition, Dr. Michael Cook, his friend and colleague, prepared a detailed biographical statement for the book. The last chapter, "Jewish-Christian Relations," is taken from Sandmel's *We Jews and You Christians,* long out of print.

There were many lay people in the auditorium, but I don't recall any other physicians who attended the symposium. During the intermission I saw Ms. Betty Bone Schiess, wife of the distinguished cardiologist Dr. William Schiess. She was one of the first women to be ordained an Episcopalian priest in the United States. When I told the Reverend Schiess that I felt somewhat out of place as a physician at such a large theological gathering, her reply was, "More of you should have come!" Later on, at the kosher or vegetarian luncheon, I was seated at the table with the black Protestant minister Reverend Emory Proctor, with the senior rabbi from Cornell University's Hillel Campus and his assistant, and with Mrs. Ramona Baxter, widow of a Unitarian minister and a religious writer for many years for the *Syracuse Post Standard*. Again, I "apologized" for attending this scholarly meeting, just being an ordinary M.D. The Senior Rabbi said I reminded him of a story, which I shall try to relate to you: It was in czarist Russia, and several prison inmates were talking to each other about the causes of their incarcerations. "I tried to assassinate the czar," the first one said. "I am here because I tried to kill the governor of a large province," the second one volunteered. "I tried unsuccessfully to get rid of a high official of the Communist Party," the third one answered. The fourth one, a meek little man, said, "I am just a thief."

"You remind me of the little thief," the Senior Rabbi continued, "but we are happy to have you. . . ."

The first speaker at the symposium was Dr. Michael Cook, from Cincinnati's Hebrew Union College. It used to be a common Christian belief, Dr. Cook told us, that the Christians had replaced the Jews as the "chosen people." The Church tried to show that Judaism is of less value by saying that the Jews were not able to accept the Hebrew Scriptures as a book that predicted Jesus Christ, and they were unable to accept the idea that Judaism is a religion of law, while Christianity is a religion of love.

According to Dr. Paul Van Buren, the Protestant second speaker, the Churches had been speaking on the subject of Christian anti-Judaism since about 1968 and had tried to eliminate those teachings. Judaism is more than a religion, Professor Van

Buren continued. "Take away a Christian's Christianity, and we have a pagan; take away a Jew's Judaism, and you have—a Jew." Just like the Jews, Van Buren dislikes the distinction between the "Old" and the "New" testaments, and he agrees with the Jews that the messianic age has not yet arrived.

Dr. Eugene Fisher, the Catholic speaker, pointed out that over the past two decades the Roman Catholic teaching materials have shown a significant improvement in the treatment of Jews and Judaism. He readily admits that the messianic age has not been achieved so far. Dr. Fisher agrees with Vatican II that Judaism is continually valid for the Jewish people.

The last speaker, Dr. Krister Stendahl, a Lutheran of Swedish descent, with a keen sense of humor, warned against the interpretation of the Old Testament God as a God of wrath, in contrast to the God of love in the New Testament. And he reminded us of Maimonides, the famous Jewish physician and philosopher who thought of Christianity *and* Islam as "Bearers of Torah to the people."

It was refreshing to learn that Jews, Christians, Moslems, and other religions have more areas of agreement than disagreement. It was, I believe, Paul Van Buren who told the meeting: "Christianity is Judaism for the Gentiles," so close are the two traditions.

Coincidences

Joan Suzanne, our daughter, had graduated from Syracuse University in Special Education. She had taken interest in that special field because of her brother's retardation. Unfortunately, when she was practice-teaching, she found that her pupils suffered more from disciplinary problems than from mental retardation. She taught second grade for two or three years in Central Square, a suburb of Syracuse, until health problems at home made it more desirable for her to spend a great deal of her time with her family. Later she became the mother of Sarah and Maurice.

Our regular lives were interrupted in 1981 by four different events. In the beginning of the year, Herta felt a tiny tissue swelling on the outside (it seemed) of her right breast. We consulted one of our surgeon friends, Dr. Daniel Burdick, who hospitalized her for one day at Crouse Irving Memorial Hospital and took a biopsy that proved the small lump to be malignant. He scheduled her for a modified radical mastectomy the following week. But, Herta didn't want to go for surgery yet, and she asked for an extended rest period before she would have to enter the hospital. It was Inge Spitz, our cousin from Toronto, who helped us out. She took three weeks off from her job and told Herta that she would come to Syracuse on the condition that Herta would enter the hospital at the specified time.

One night, after visiting Herta at the hospital, Inge and I were watching television, reading, and talking at the same time. I have become quite an expert at looking at the television and reading a most interesting book at the same time. (The only thing

I have in common with Albert Einstein is the fact that the professor was the only person in Princeton who couldn't understand a football game.) I pointed out to Inge that it was very good of Mrs. Gerald Ford and Mrs. Nelson Rockefeller to talk so frankly about their own mastectomies. I also spoke of Hildegard Knef, the German actress who, after the war, had performed in some American movies and Broadway stage shows. She had written about her own breast cancer in the book *The Verdict*. At the very moment I said that, Merv Griffin announced his next guest, "And now, Hildegard Knef." She was on one of her visits to the States, and she performed some songs on Griffin's show that evening. I thought that I had developed something of a sixth sense, and I immediately thought of our encounter with Peter Hurkos.

Herta, myself, Mel, Joan, and some of our California relatives saw Mr. Hurkos, the clairvoyant, quite a few years ago at Syracuse's Three Rivers Inn. Many famous Hollywood and Broadway performers have performed there at one time or another. Once Mike Douglas had his picture taken with our Michael, and Joan Rivers autographed a picture for him. That evening Peter Hurkos asked the audience for some not visible, covered objects which he would then try to identify with his touch. Herta held in her hand a picture of Michael, wrapped in a paper so that it was impossible to see the photograph. The psychic came over, touched the small print, and said to her, "This is someone you love very much, but you cannot help him as much as you would like to." At that moment, his face started to perspire, he seemed shaken up, and he told our group and the large audience, "I cannot go on, I shall be back later." When he returned after this intermission, he continued his performance. "Your mother died on a Friday," he said to Herta, "but you don't know where and when." (She had died in a Nazi concentration camp.) "You will have three," he pointed to Mel and Joan, who are the parents of two at this time, but had no offspring as yet at the time of Hurkos's act. But the real surprise was what he said to Mel, "You were in Bangkok, Thailand." Not too many servicemen had ever been to that particular city, but in the early 1960s Mel had been stationed in Vietnam and later in Korea, and on one of his rare furloughs he had been able to visit the picturesque city of Bangkok. The performer was right when he predicted that Herta would have a lot of problems with her left leg. She certainly has. Aside from pain radiating from her degenerative disk, she had marked edema and chronic dermatitis in her left lower extremity.

One of my former patients, Ms. Lorraine Doddy, happened to be waiting on tables at Three Rivers Inn that night. Ms. Doddy offered to introduce me to Peter Hurkos. She did. "Isn't it true, Doctor," he asked, "I didn't know you, and you didn't know me?" I had to agree.

Hurkos had been called in as a psychic expert in the Boston Strangler case, his biography was published in 1970 by Doubleday, and I have in front of me a 1973 newspaper interview of him. He revealed in this conversation with the *Enquirer* his "most memorable psychic experience." The clipping was sent to me by our California relatives, who had been with us at "our" show. You know where his most memorable experience in July 1971 took place? At Syracuse's Three Rivers Inn, of course. A woman in the audience handed him an envelope with a photograph in it. Peter Hurkos told the lady that the man in the photo had been whipped to death in a World War II concentration camp. The woman was astonished at how accurate he was. When Hurkos went into all the details, he could not go on any longer and had to leave the stage. At the same time, the article said, he was perspiring, clammy, and developed bloody red marks all over his body, reliving the prisoner's experience. A physician in the audience, Dr. James Grant of Oswego, examined him later and was able to verify all of the psychic's bodily changes. All this came back to my mind while I was watching Hildegard Knef on the "Merv Griffin Show."

Herta returned from the hospital after her mastectomy, and she is checked at regular intervals by Dr. Burdick, her surgeon. She has also had a number of radiation treatments administered by Dr. Pankay Dalal at Upstate Medical Center. Naturally, I added to my library several books written by cancer patients. All of them show an excellent knowledge of the subject. Some of the books I have read; some I use as a reference. I have mentioned

The Verdict by Hildegard Knef. I also have Dr. Samuel Sanes's *A Physician Faces Cancer in Himself.* Another book by a physician is *Recalled By Life* by Anthony Sattillaro, M.D. He was about 47 years old when he was stricken with cancer of the prostrate gland. He was treated with extensive surgery and drug therapy, but metastatic lesions had spread through his ribcage and all over his body. With the permission of his doctors, he went on a strange vegetarian diet. To his and his doctors' surprise, these lesions disappeared whenever he stuck to this strange diet, and they returned whenever he got off it. To the best of my recollection, I have never found a review of Dr. Sattillaro's story in any of my medical periodicals except in *M.D.* magazine. One of the most well-known accounts of a breast cancer history was published almost a decade ago by Betty Rollin, a television news reporter, under the title *First You Cry.* At about the same time, *Why Me?* a very learned book written by cancer survivor Rose Kushner came out.

One of the most recent additions to the field is Rena Blumberg's *Headstrong.* This lady had undergone a mastectomy as well as aggressive chemotherapy, and her book shows much psychological insight. One of the reasons that I became attracted to Mrs. Blumburg's book was the recommendation given it by Norman Cousins, former editor of the *Saturday Review* and a professor of law and human values at the University of California in Los Angeles. In his book, *Anatomy of an Illness,* he showed us that he was able to overcome a crippling, almost incurable disease just with his positive, optimistic attitude. In a more recent and still more convincing volume, *The Healing Heart,* he describes his victory over a most serious heart attack. He had some of the best cardiologists as his doctors, of course, but they listened to him as an intelligent layman, and sometimes he was able to sway their opinions. And always, his *will to live* shines through. The gist of Cousin's essays is his conviction that psychological factors can influence the outcome of disease. There is a beautiful introduction to Cousin's book by Dr. Bernard Lown, professor of cardiology at Harvard. He agrees with Cousins that a good humanistic education is a very important factor in the selection of medical students, and he stresses the significance of communications between doctor and patients. Through numerous examples he shows that words can kill and words can give life.

Another event took place in 1981: a pleasant one. I attended the wedding of Jenny Preuss, daughter of Fred Preuss, a friend from my Breslau school days. He was working as a pathologist in Dallas at the time, and he and his wife Sonja invited me to San Antonio, where the ceremony was held. Both Jenny and her fiance, Chris Ticknor, had gone to San Antonio Medical College and intended to specialize in psychiatry. Mr. Ticknor came from a refined family of Christian background and did not formally convert to Judaism, but he readily agreed to be married by a Rabbi. Jenny's former Sunday School teacher, Rabbi Jack Bemporad, consented to come from Dallas to perform the wedding ceremony.

I had read articles and book reviews by Rabbi Bemporad for a long time, and it was a pleasure to be able to converse with him at the wedding reception. At that time I had just been reading *The Parnas* by Silvano Arieti, famous psychiatrist and psychoanalyst and editor of the *American Handbook of Psychiatry*. In the book, the Parnas, or elder of the Jewish community, suffered from a severe emotional disease but finally gained complete insight into his mental illness before he died, a martyr, at the hands of the Nazis. I had no idea that Dr. Arieti was an Italian Jew who had left his home town of Pisa in 1939 to escape the Nazis. Dr. Arieti returned to Pisa a few years after his emigration in order to interview any survivors he could find. His small volume is one of the most moving stories I have ever read. About a year after *The Parnas* came out, Arieti's last book, *Abraham and the Contemporary Mind,* appeared. I was astonished at the author's profound knowledge not only of psychiatric topics, but also of Judaism, history, and general philosophy.

Knowing that Rabbi Bemporad came from an Italian Jewish family, I asked him if he was familiar with Arieti's *The Parnas*. "He is a cousin of mine," he replied. Not only that, but the rabbi's brother, psychiatrist Jules Bemporad, M.D., coauthored a book with Silvano Arieti, *Severe and Mild Depression.* Unfortunately, the rabbi continued, Dr. Arieti had been stricken with a fatal disease. Quite soon after the wedding, I saw a little obituary note in the *New York State Journal of Medicine,* but, to my dismay, I was unable to find any detailed article in any of the leading medical or psychotherapeutic journals devoted to this great man—one of the leading psychiatrists in the U.S. and the world. I could not help wondering whether official psychiatry considers a psychiatrist "off the mainstream" as soon as he talks about religious ideas or searches with his patients and the general public for the meaning of life. As mentioned before, Viktor Frankl's *Search for Meaning* has been omitted from many psychiatric textbooks.

    I would have loved to continue my conversation with Rabbi Bemporad, but Chris's relatives, proud inhabitants of San Antonio, were most anxious to show the rabbi the sights of their beautiful city. He happily accepted. The night before the wedding, at a dinner for relatives and friends, I expressed my hope that the young couple's marital happiness should last at least as long as my sixty-year-old friendship to Jenny's father Fred. Jenny and Chris are both psychiatric residents now, and I have no doubt that everything will be all right in their common future.

The third event affecting me in 1981 was a relatively minor and benign one. After my first home-office combination, I had moved to the Medical Arts Building where I practiced for about a dozen years. Eventually the name of the building had been changed, and three of the six floors had been converted into efficiency apartments. In September 1981 I changed my location to the State Tower, one of the most prestigious buildings in the city of Syracuse. There I still am, on the 16th floor of the 21-story building, overlooking the city—the nicest office I have ever had. Ms. Joan Wallace, the building manager, was most helpful in selecting the proper office with me. There are stores, a cafeteria, and a newsstand in the building. My office is located between the consultation rooms of two eminent psychiatrists: Dr. Aron Arnow and Dr. Robert Seidenberg. Dr. Arnow, originally from Europe, has worked for years at the Menninger Clinic. His wife is a psychological counselor in the same building. Dr. Seidenberg is the author of several books, including *Marriage in Life and Literature, Corporate Wives-Corporate Casualties,* and his most recent one, *Women Who Marry Houses,* which details the causes and treatment of agoraphobia. Right next to me is the busy investment office of J. W. Burns & Co., which intrigues me no end as I never knew anything about stocks and bonds. Across the hall from me was the surgical practice facility of Dr. Bernard Piskor, who passed away due to a cardiac condition close to two years ago. I have never heard of so many grateful patients mourn their beloved physician as in the case of Dr. Piskor. His office is now occupied by two young attorneys, Greenwald & Dague, very fine people both of whom are a credit to our building. Moving to another location at that stage of life was a lot of work, of course, but it was for me—in retrospect—a favorable event.

The fourth occurrence in 1981, though, was a traumatic one. It was a Thursday in mid-October when I dropped Mel off in front of an office building on East Jefferson Street. I started to back my 1977 Buick Skylark out of the parking spot and noticed that the motor was racing. I went forward, and the same thing happened. I was unable to control the vehicle. My main concern was not to hit anybody as the street was fairly busy at the time. The automobile veered to the left, and I decided to crash into a pillar in back of Sibley's Department Store. The pillar was not hurt, but I was. I had pains in my ribcage and some bleeding from my nose and mouth. One kind bystander came over with a clean, white handkerchief. I did not even have a chance to thank him. The ambulance was there in no time, but I convinced them that nothing was broken and that I had an appointment with Dr. Grossman that afternoon anyway. Mel, my son-in-law, had heard the crash and came down fast from the office building. I explained to him that I would like to have the car repaired as soon as possible in order to get back to work. "The car is a total loss," he told me, and he was right.

I found one of my encounters that day very touching: A young black man with a small beard, a former patient, cried out, "I don't want him to get hurt; he is my doctor!" I looked his record up—I had not seen him for eight years, and I have never seen him since.

I was sitting with the police officer when he made out his report. He did not give me a ticket, and he listed mechanical failure as the cause of the accident. One minor detail had yet to be taken care of. There was blood all over my face, and there were blood spots on my shirt. I had to get rid of the evidence to prevent Herta from getting too upset. Mel borrowed a friend's car and drove me to his friend's home, which is close to ours, and I washed up to the best of my ability. Herta was not fooled, but she calmed down when she realized that I was not hurt too seriously. It took me a while, though, to overcome the initial shock and to feel able to drive again. The car was a total loss. The Kemper Insurance Company was very fair in reimbursing me at the prevailing rate when the time came to replace the demolished car with a new one.

Syracuse: City of Diversity

Syracuse is one of the few cities in the United States where an organization like the Syracuse Area Interreligious Council exists. Founded by Rabbi Theodore Levy, its large membership consists of representatives of Catholicism, Protestantism, and Judaism, as well as Islamism, Bahaism, and other denominations. One of the most active members of this organizations was Dr. Darrell Fasching, who now works as a professor of religious studies at the University of South Florida in Tampa. He comes from a Catholic background, and I am lucky enough to hear from him from time to time. He sent me a copy of his most recent paper, entitled *Can Christian Faith Survive Auschwitz?*. There is nothing in this study that a Jew cannot wholeheartedly agree with, and it is a hopeful sign indeed to know that so much more unites than divides us.

For the past three years, another group has met regularly in Syracuse to discuss the prospects of real peace in the Middle East. The group consists of twenty-one people: seven Jews, seven Muslim and Christian Palestinians, and seven American Christians. After a difficult start, they were able to put a consensus statement together. Similar dialogue groups are planned for Rochester, Chicago, Baltimore, Washington, D.C., and San Francisco. But again—the start was made in Syracuse.

Recently, there was a report in the Syracuse newspapers about a fund drive that had been started by our own Syracuse Area Interreligious Council for the victims of starvation in Ethiopia. All the organizations sponsored by our Catholic, Protestant, and Jewish communities participated. No questions were asked about dogma or belief; what counted was practical, social action. The present president of the Interreligious Council is Barry Silverberg, publisher of the *Jewish Observer;* Michael Moss, a former president of Temple Society of Concord, is on its Board of Directors.

What is this city's religious understanding and brotherhood due to? This is the seat of Syracuse University with its ideals of liberty and tolerance. For about the last twenty years, Rabbi Milton Elefant has been the very active elder of Syracuse University's large Hillel Student Foundation. Decades ago, at one of the local synagogues, a debate was held between the late Dean of Hendricks Chapel, Charles Noble, who spoke about "Jesus, the Christian," and Professor Fred Krinsky of the Political Science Department and chairman of the Jewish Student Fellowship, whose theme was "Jesus, the Jew." Both speakers agreed from the start that Jesus was a Jew, a simple fact that was overlooked by the Nazis as well as by the totalitarian regime of Ayatollah Khomeini.

Whoever is caught in our college's liberal, interdenominational spirit is affected by it. It was in the 1950s that I rented part of my driveway to a postgraduate student who had been sent, with many others, by the Venezuelan government to take business administration courses at the University. We lived on South Salina Street then, and for the past thirty years we have received each Christmas and New Year a beautiful card and message from Carlos B. Contreras and his large family in Caracas. Two or three years ago, we got a telephone call from Dorothy Niazi, who was a tenant in our house when we resided in the inner city. Her husband, Dr. Suad Niazi, who practices in Minnesota, was born in Iraq; she, American born, is a born-again Christian. We have unfortunately lost track of Dr. and Mrs. Aidun, who both, as I remember, had left their native Iran to escape persecution for their belief in the Bahai religion. They lived in India until he came to serve an internship at Syracuse's General Hospital. Whenever Mrs. Aidun had a chance, she helped with our son Michael. They took me along sometimes to their Bahai social meetings. A delightful group of people, a wonderful couple!

My own neighborhood in DeWitt is made up of people from many very different backgrounds. I already knew some of them from South Salina Street: Mr. John Gorman, the real estate agent, sold me the house on South Salina Street in 1945 and our house in DeWitt; he was also a patient of mine. The late Mr. Gorman is the father of Ms. King, whose family lives on our block in DeWitt. Mrs. Carol Wandner also lived on our street then. Her parents owned Richman's College Inn, a landmark in Syracuse, next to the Regent Theater. For a while Mrs. Wandner was host for the "Jewish Journal" on television and now she is on the advisory committee for the *Syracuse Jewish Observer.*

We found on our small DeWitt street whites and blacks, Gentiles and Jews, people from all different races, religions, and cultures. Among our neighbors are Mr. Clark, whose wife, although elderly, takes care of babies and small children whenever parents in the neighborhood need her services; Mrs. Walter McMullen, whose husband died about a year ago due to a treacherous illness; Mr. Anthony Vergara and his wife, who gave us a small kitten that had come to their house since she had six already. We called the kitten Raquel, and she is still with us. Next to Mel, Joan, and our grandchildren lives the Collins family with their daughter Chikina, who plays with Sarah and Maurice.

Across the street from us resides Louis DeStefano, owner of a roofing company, with his wife Jenny. Both come from an Italian-Catholic background; the lady is a saint who cannot do enough for her family or others. She explained to us once that she came from a large family of thirteen. When we asked if her husband Louis also came from such a large family, she answered, "Oh, no—only nine." Next to the DeStefanos live Mr. and Mrs. Steve Porter with their little daughter Lisa. Whenever Mr. Porter is asked for help by some neighbors, he is there; Mrs. Porter is an artist.

The Doss family on the other side of the street came from India and are Christians, while the Costas are of Italian background, I believe. Dr. Nabil El Hassan, a gynecologist from Lebanon, has moved closer to Community Hospital, while his parents, his sister Haifa, and her daughter Marva—a playmate of my grandchildren—now occupy the doctor's house on our street. They all profess the Muslim faith. It is always a pleasure for me to talk with Mr. El Hassan Sr., a retired judge with a well-rounded education, who, unfortunately, has very poor eyesight now. Just last night my daughter Joan received a telephone call from her friend Liang Wong. She and her husband Chun Fook Wong, a biochemist at Upstate Medical Center, had come to the United States from Singapore. Their children, Ginger and Clinton, went to school with Sarah and Maurice. For several years now, Mr. Wong has been working for the large Abbott Pharmaceutical Company at North Chicago, Illinois. Since they moved from our street, Mrs. Liang communicates with us about once a month.

There is a common humanity that binds us all. We are proud to live in a neighborhood and city where people of so many different backgrounds like each other and live together in peace.

Second Career

I had never written a book until this one. I have contributed, though, many "letters to the editors" of a variety of medical, Jewish, and general magazines. Once I wrote a letter in response to the distinguished editor of *Modern Medicine,* Dr. Walter C. Alvarez. I have also sent letters to our local Onondaga County Medical Society *Bulletin* and to the internationally known *Medical Tribune.* Others were published by *Aufbau, Commentary Magazine,* and, in recent years, the *Syracuse Herald American* and the *Syracuse Jewish Observer.*

It was the *Jewish Observer,* though, that gave me a new, second career. For years the Syracuse Jewish Federation had published a small paper; the *Observer* was at first a monthly paper, but for a number of years has been published every two weeks. Its editor, Mrs. Sherry Chayat, is the daughter of the late renowned sculptor, Maxwell Chayat. She was director of public relations at LeMoyne College when she was appointed chief editor of the *Syracuse Jewish Observer.* I couldn't help noticing the quality of the paper and the progress it made. So, I wrote a letter to the editor in February 1982 explaining that I was delighted with the *Observer*—its editorial content, its readers' communications—but that I missed the regular review of Jewish books. Before my letter was published with editorial comment, the editor wrote me personally to ask if I would be interested in reporting about Jewish lectures or other events of Jewish interest or if I would be interested in writing some book reviews myself. She added that the *Jewish Observer* had only a small, voluntary staff. I was grateful for the chance to work on something so important for me.

I had recently attended a lecture sponsored by the Syracuse Area Interreligious Council held at Hendrick's Chapel. It was the fourth and last one in a series about "faith today," and the speaker was Professor John Stoessinger, an agnostic of Jewish heritage, a humanist who was born and raised in Vienna. He was introduced by his friend, the Rev. Dr. Richard Phillips, Dean of Hendrick's Chapel. The professor, who had learned as a child about the miraculous Exodus from Egypt, and, on the other hand, survived the tragedy of the Holocaust, felt unable to believe in a personal God anymore. His talk and the following discussion were most impressive. I am sure that the Dean and a large part of the audience had a different interpretation of the Bible and of religious faith than did this non-theologian. But he was able to state his views without censorship, as was only to be expected in this city of Syracuse. My short review and report on Stoessinger's lecture was the only one I did on lecture meetings; from then on I concentrated on book reviews.

I used to purchase my books directly from the publishers, or from the medical bookstore at the Upstate Medical Center, but mostly from the Economy Bookstore. Whenever a volume was not available locally, they would order it for me. Years ago, the Otisco Book and Gift Shop, owned by Mrs. Sarah Rosenbloom, specialized in Judaica. In the past two or three decades, Jewish books have begun to be read more and more by the general public; some of them have even been on best seller lists and, therefore, have been obtainable from any good bookstore. For many years, though, Mrs. Rosenbloom's Otisco Book and Gift Shop was a Jewish landmark in Syracuse, and she seemed somewhat disappointed that she was not included in the otherwise excellent Rudolph book on Jews in Syracuse.

Once I started to write book reviews, I was pleased to receive free review copies right from the publishers. My very first reports, though, were on books I had purchased for my own personal library. The first one, I recall, was Marie Jastrow's *A Time To Remember*. Mrs. Jastrow, the mother of the famous astrophysicist Robert Jastrow, wrote this, her first book, at the age of about eighty-one. In an interview by Herbert Mitgang from the *New York Times,* the scientist referred to Mrs. Jastrow as "my mother, the author."

The Jewish Soul on Fire by Esther Jungreis was the next book I discussed. A powerful speaker of Orthodox Jewish persuasion, she was trying to help lost souls to find their Jewish identity but never set out to convert gentiles. What impressed me most was her ability to communicate on university campuses with leaders of the so-called Hebrew-Christians, who were only waiting for a chance to return to their fold. These poor souls, still considered Jews by main-line Christians, go to their own synagogues. About two thousand years ago there existed a small Jewish group, the Jewish Christians, who believed with the Gentile followers of Jesus of Nazareth that the messianic age was at hand. Later, when the split came between Judaism and the new daughter religion, they had to decide whether to be Jewish or Christian; you can't be both. The Jews remained apart, in spite of persecutions. The Catholic Church, through the Inquisition, tried forceful conversion, and Martin Luther, the Protestant Reformer, was unsuccessful with friendly persuasion and later became violently anti-Semitic. While most Jews suffered persecutions but refused to abandon their beliefs, a few made the unsuccessful compromise of becoming Hebrew-Christians. Now, of course, Jews, Christians, Moslems, Buddhists, and Hindus may get together in organizations like our Syracuse Area Interreligious Council and soon find out that more things unite than divide us. It isn't easy, though, to get all the people together for this great task of understanding, especially those of fundamentalist faiths. It will never be possible to sit down with somebody like Ayatollah Khomeini to talk about brotherhood.

Some of the other books I reviewed were Paul Cowan's *An Orphan in History, Choosing Judaism* by Lydia Kukoff, who came from an Italian Baptist family and converted to Judaism, *The Nine Questions People Ask About Judaism* by Dennis Prager and Joseph Telushkin, and even some fiction by Cynthia Ozick. There was the scholarly book, *The Springs of Jewish Life,* authored by Chaim Raphael, a British-Jewish writer. More of my reviews are yet to be printed, like *The Making of Modern Zionism* by Shlomo Avineri, and two paperbacks by Steinsaltz, *The Essential Talmud* and *Biblical Images*. Another little book review of mine, not published as yet, is on the *World Guide for the Jewish Traveler*, a delightful paperback put out by Dutton Publishing Company. Another most important volume I reported on, which I still consider to be outstanding, is *Jews and Christians After the Holocaust*, published by the Fortress Press. I also reviewed Dr. Claudine Vegh's *I Didn't Say Goodbye* based on interviews this psychiatrist had with French Jews who had lost one or both parents in the Holocaust.

Of all the books I reviewed, though, I loved best the biography of Martin Buber written by Maurice Friedman, now professor of religious studies and philosophy at San Diego State University. *Martin Buber's Life and Work* consists of three large volumes covering the whole of Buber's life, starting with his early years and ending at the time of his passing in 1965, when he was close to the age of 90. For me, who had heard Buber speak once before my emigration from Breslau, it was fascinating to read about the Jewish philosopher's life and work in Israel, his writings, his huge correspondence with the greatest men and women all over the world, his guest lectures in the United States and Europe, and the numerous awards and prizes he earned. True, Buber is not always easy for the average person to understand, but Friedman's book brings him much closer to us. My enthusiasm for the remarkable biography must have shown—I was happy to find a sentence from my review reprinted in the *Dutton News* of April 1984, between a quote from the *Library Journal* and the *San Francisco Chronicle*. I was also very pleased to receive an invitation by Ms. Janet Kraybill of Dutton's publicity department to meet with Maurice Friedman, the author, while he was in New York this past September. Unfortunately, I was unable to make it.

One reason I was able to identify with Buber so much is our common German-Jewish heritage. Therefore, I subtitled this book, "The Memoirs of a German-Jewish Immigrant Physician."

Let me quote a summary of Buber's ideas, as he expressed them in one of the discussion groups he held while lecturing in America:

> There are things in the Jewish tradition I cannot accept at all, and things I hold true that are not expressed in Judaism. But what I hold essential has been expressed more in biblical Judaism than anywhere else in the biblical dialogue between man and God. . . . I want to show that Judaism can be lived. It is most important that the Jews today live Judaism.

I cannot wait to review a book soon to be published by Basic Books. *Strangers In Their Own Land: Young Jews in Germany and Austria Today,* by Peter Sichrovsky, describes the younger generation of Jews in today's Germany whose parents survived the Nazi concentration camps. They all were born in Germany or Austria after 1945.

I have also been reading quite a few interesting books lately. A few months ago, Dr. Sol Gordon, professor of child and family studies at Syracuse University, spoke before a large audience at the Temple Society of Concord about his newest book *When Living Hurts.* He autographed my copy afterward and was pleased to learn that my autobiographical story is being published by Prometheus. "The editor [Paul Kurtz]," he said, "is a friend of mine." He talks in his little volume about suicide and suicide prevention, especially in teenagers, and asks everybody to reach out to the lonely, depressed, and discouraged, to be compassionate, and to convince them that they have friends. This is in contrast to some psychiatric teachers who would not interfere with the patient's suicide plans unless the patient asks for help.

A very powerful book is Alice Kaminsky's *The Victim's Song,* published by Prometheus. The author's twenty-two-year-old son Eric was slain by criminals on New York's subway tracks. He was her and her husband's only child. A professor of English at Cortland College, Alice Kaminsky shows that the justice system feels more pity for the criminal than for the victim or the potential victim, and she tries to understand philosophically and religiously the fate of her son and countless others. This valiant lady continues to teach, but her main goal in life is to keep her son's memory alive.

I am presently absorbed in the biography of Edith Stein by Waltraud Herbstrith, translated by Bernard Bonowitz. I found the book just recently on the Judaica shelf of Economy Bookstore. What is so strange about this book is the fact that Edith Stein was a nun, a Jewish nun. What a coincidence it is that her parents had moved from Posen to Breslau, where Edith was born. My parents also moved to Breslau after I was born in Ostrow in the Posen Province. From the age of thirteen to age twenty-one, Edith was unable to believe in a personal God. She studied philosophy and mysticism and gradually felt drawn to the Catholic faith. She was baptized in 1922, an act her mother and most of her large family could not comprehend. They continued to love her, recognizing her honesty and deep conviction. When Edith later joined a Carmelite order in Cologne, the whole family felt crushed. Her 84-year-old mother did not get angry; she just cried. Like all converts to other religions in Jewish history, Edith Stein always stressed that she was a Jewess. She kept in contact with her family to the bitter end, and she prayed for her Jewish brothers and sisters when the Nazi laws came into effect. She was taken from her Dutch convent to Auschwitz, where she died in 1942. She persisted in the religious idea that the Lord had called on her to suffer a sacrificial death to help the Jewish people, just as Queen Esther was called upon in the Old Testament—an idea that no Jewish person can accept.

What made Edith Stein's story so personal for me is the fact that she was born and raised in Breslau, Germany, my own home town. Also, one of her sisters, Dr. Erna Biberstein, was able to get to the United States in the nick of time and practiced gynecology in New York for a number of years. Her husband, Professor Hans Biberstein, taught and practiced dermatology. I still remember him slightly.

Books can be so important to people. Just recently Anatoly Shcharansky, second-most famous political prisoner (after Andrei Sakharov), was released from a Soviet prison. When interviewed by reporters in Israel, he talked about the small book of Hebrew psalms his wife Avital had sent him while he was incarcerated. At one time he'd had to spend 130 days in solitary confinement because he had gone on a hunger strike when prison guards wanted to confiscate the book. It was religious literature, they said, which is forbidden to Soviet inmates. When he was going to be released from his labor camp, his escorts tried again to confiscate the books of psalms. He told them that he would not leave the country without the psalms, "which helped me so much. I lay down in the snow and said, NOT ANOTHER STEP." So, the guards examined the bindings, "presumably for hidden material," he said, and returned it. How stubborn can one get! On the other hand, Shcharansky would not have been so lucky had he been confronted by Nazi guards.

Ms. Sherry Chayat, who gave me a second career by letting me do book reviews, is now editor emeritus, although she still writes guest editorials from time to time. She has been an art critic for the *Syracuse Herald Journal* and *Herald American* since her retirement from the *Jewish Observer,* and she will teach an art course this spring at Syracuse's University College.

The *Jewish Observer* was lucky to find a replacement for Sherry Chayat in Ms. Judith Rubenstein, who had been her assistant editor for quite some time. Ms. Rubenstein printed a letter that I had written at the time of the passing of Dr. Harry Feldman, professor of preventive medicine at Upstate Medical College, who had discovered with Albert Sabin the Sabin-Feldman die test for the diagnosis of toxoplasmosis. This able and efficient journalist also published my review of Maurice Friedman's third and final volume of his biography of Buber, and I was pleased to learn that some readers purchased the set after learning about it from my book report.

Grandchildren

My grandchildren Sarah, age 14, and Maurice, almost 12, are really getting along nicely. When Joan, Sarah's mother, went to the hospital to deliver her next baby with help of Dr. Robert Hays, her obstetrician, Sarah specifically asked for a baby sister. But, now both Sarah and Maurice are content with their roles in life, and they get along splendidly.

Sarah gets good grades in school, but her mind is all made up. She wants to be a fashion designer. She also likes to write soap opera stories. She can cook and bake, and she is able to put broken things together quickly.

Both Sarah and Maurice have to be coaxed to attend Sunday School at the local synagogue. Maurice takes Hebrew School lessons, for he wants to become a Bar Mitzvah. It is strange, but even reputable Hebrew scholars confess that they never liked to attend Sunday School classes; somehow they make up for it later.

Both grandchildren take German in school, and I am glad they do. After all, Germany had been a country of poets and thinkers—until the dark ages of the thousand year Reich swept over it. I would like for them to be able to read some of the books I own that are written in German, which are of lasting value.

Right now, Sarah is far away from reading those books (as is Maurice). She, the future fashion designer, knows how to dress. If somebody remarks to her, "Sarah, don't you look nice today?" her stock answer is, "I know it." Yet, she is loyal and dependable. She always stays in contact with her friends. Aside from her friends in school, like Tina Harrison, Sonia Wilkins, and Jessica

Davis, whom she sees on a daily basis, she keeps in contact by mail or phone with those who have moved to or live in other states. As a matter of fact, she is the only one in the family, aside from me, who writes letters. She corresponds with Ginger Wong in North Chicago, with her cousin Sheri in Toronto, and she often speaks on the phone to her friend Michelle Graham, who moved to Arizona last year. I wonder sometimes if losing the art of letter writing is not deplorable. If a doctor (here we go again) sends a patient to a specialist, he does not want a phone call reporting on the patient but wants a comprehensive written record, which will have a lasting value for years to come. How could the biographers of Siegmund Freud, Franz Kafka, Albert Einstein, Leo Tolstoy, or Fyodor Dostoevsky ever have performed their tasks if they had not had access to correspondence? So, I am glad that Sarah continues to write to her friends like Kelly Fairbanks, who just moved to one of Syracuse's other suburbs.

How loving Sarah is. On Valentine's Day 1986, she had a picture of our beautiful kitten, Raquel, enlarged and gold-framed by one of the nearby photo labs to give as a gift to Herta. Joan intended to pick the gift up on her way back from taking Herta to the doctor. It was shortly before the five o'clock closing time, and Sarah's mother hadn't returned. Sarah walked through snow and ice the few blocks to the photo lab and got the framed print out just in the nick of time. Sarah also makes sure that grandmother takes her medication, and she reads stories to Michael, if he does not feel so well, for hours at a time, while Raquel lies down on his bed.

Another love in Sarah's life is our dog Rusty, a mixture of wire-haired terrier and dachshund, I believe. Nobody is sure about his age, but it is somewhere around nineteen. Rusty was between two and three years old when he jumped into Mel's car at the University branch of Lincoln Bank. He has never left us since, in spite of our trying to find the rightful owner. When we were visited by Esther, daughter of our friend Rita Seligman, she saw Rusty eating and wagging his tail happily and said to him the golden words, "You have got it made." Once, many summers ago, Michael was sitting outside on our lawn at an umbrella table, when that umbrella began to collapse, endangering Michael. Rusty started to bark and ran forth and back between the table and the house until he got the attention of Eleene, who removed the threat. Eleene, who had never had much experience with pets before, loves Rusty and Raquel.

We all continue to learn from Michael, but he has had an especially good influence on Sarah and Maurice. He loves people genuinely, whether they are rich or poor. He is satisfied with what he has and appreciates small things in life. He has given all the people who have taken care of him meaning in their lives. He idolizes our grandchildren and is extremely happy if they sit with him and read to him. Sarah and Maurice have learned through Michael to be good to and understanding of all people and to relate to the handicapped. The reader might remember that their Aunt Lucy played the piano every year for the elderly at the Jewish Home for the Aged and the Ida Benderson Home; Sarah and Maurice sang and danced for them.

Maurice says that he would like to go into medicine, and none of us would mind. He watches while I draw the insulin into the syringe for his grandmother, and once he did it himself. He makes sure that Grandma follows her diet and observes if her legs are swollen. Quite some years ago, Michael was sitting in the sun and, possibly due to the heat or some allergy, suffered small seizures, petit mals, with short unconscious spells and shaking movements. Maurice, who had never seen anything like that before, ran to the house and told Eleene: "Hurry, Aunt Eleene! Uncle Mike is trying to run away."

Another time Maurice saw some jelly beans and other candy on the table in front of Eleene, and he admonished her to mash those jelly beans up before she gave them to Michael, knowing that Michael had lost his teeth.

When Maurice was quite small, he played with his little friend of Chinese extraction, Clinton Wong, now in North Chicago. They played very well together; but, apparently, Clinton's English vocabulary was not too big yet, as I remember Maurice asking, "Can't he talk a little bit?"

My mind goes back to the time when Joan was a little girl.

Joan was fed by her mother a little too long, it seems, and the portions appeared too big to me. "You can't sit all day long," our pediatrician friend Robert Schwartz told Herta. "Take it away after twenty minutes if she does not eat." History repeats itself: When Maurice was a small boy, he felt unable to eat everything on his plate. On one occasion he blurted out, "Don't you know I have only a little stomach?"

Maurice does not play an instrument, although he took piano for a while with Sarah when they were both quite a bit younger. He has not been sticking to his guitar lessons either so far, but he has not given up yet. Sarah's good friend Tina Houser has been playing the flute for some time, so Sarah went back to her piano lessons and seems to mean it this time. She might even persuade her brother to follow her lead in the selection of an instrument.

Maurice's friends' families come from various educational backgrounds. Danny Renaud's father is in the car business. Jack Sugarman's father is an orthopedic surgeon, and Cary Devorsetz's father is an attorney. Kenny Porter is the grandson of our late friend, Dr. Hans Seligman. Matt Warshal Liddle, the son of Dick and Donna Liddle, sees Maurice frequently after school. Mr. Liddle is one of the vice presidents of Key Bank. Gary Slagle is the son of a mathematics teacher, while alen Webster's father teaches orthopedic surgery at Upstate Medical Center. I hope that all these boys will remember each other fondly after a period of sixty or seventy years as I remember those who had gone to school with me.

I have had the opportunity to help Maurice with Hebrew and German lessons sometimes. He promised, in turn, to teach me computer science at some time in the future. I remember that I told him the story of Diogenes, the Greek philosopher who went during the bright noon hour to the marketplace in Athens, carrying a big lantern with him. When asked by bystanders what he was doing, he replied, "I am looking for an honest man." He lived in a barrel, and his only possession was his drinking cup. When he saw a small boy standing by the river and drinking out of his hand, Diogenes threw his cup away. No need to bother anymore with such an unimportant item as a cup! King Croesus, who was very wealthy, approached the philosopher. "Make a wish, and your request will be granted," he said. The wise old man did not think too long before he replied, "Please, your Majesty, get out of the sun!" And King Croesus's answer was, "If I were not Croesus, I would love to be Diogenes."

Maurice's reaction to the story was, "This guy Diogenes seems stupid to me." I was a little shocked at first about my grandson's harsh judgment. But, come to think of it, nobody today can imitate Diogenes's lifestyle. Who could live in a barrel in our climate in zero degree weather? We are all dependent upon machines. While writing this book, I am using my electric Smith Corona typewriter with interchangeable ribbon cartridges, and I would not know what to do without my dependable small Sharp photocopier. We also know that the economy would collapse if everybody stopped buying anything but the barest essentials. What Diogenes had in mind was, "If you don't have it, get along without it!" And he didn't have very much. But, with grandchildren like I have, Diogenes would feel like a rich man.

Seventieth Birthday Party

The outstanding event for me in 1983 was my seventieth birthday party, arranged by my family, held at the Marriott Inn, and taped and videotaped. My actual birthday was in May, but some of the invited guests were unable to make it then, so we scheduled the celebration for the 18th of June. Still, a few of my friends could not attend. My good friend from Breslau school days, Dr. Fred Preuss, was in the process of moving from Dallas to San Antonio, and Dr. Franz Josef Nave, school physician for the city of Cincinnati, was visiting Germany at the time. My classmate Felix Taucher from Joplin, Missouri, had unfortunately passed away over a year before due to severe heart disease. Yet, two other co-pupils from the early grades of Breslau's Koenig Wilhelm Gymnasium were there: Ken Walton and Erwin Zadik.

Ken Walton's original name used to be Wartenberger, and his late father was a cantor at Breslau's Neue Synagogue. After attending the lowest grades with me at our humanistic gymnasium where the teaching of Greek and Latin predominated, his parents moved him to the Zwinger Gymnasium where more practical subjects prevailed. I had not heard anything about Ken Wartenberger until I saw an announcement in *Aufbau* many years ago about the passing of his father. I sent him my condolences, and he sent me a very cordial letter by return mail. That was in the 1960s. Then he telephoned me in Syracuse, where his only son Ralph attended Syracuse's Upstate Medical Center. Ken, himself, had a position as manager of the nationally known Gem Store. I have seen him and his wonderful Paula at regular intervals ever since.

The first time we met after our childhood days was at my Syracuse office. He exclaimed, "My God, have we changed!" He and Paula finally moved back to Rochester, New York, where they once lived, and where his brother and family live.

Through Ken and Paula we also again met Kurt and Thea Silverstein, formerly from Breslau, now also living in Rochester. When Herta was a nurse, she had taken care of their son Peter while he was a very sick baby at the Breslau Jewish Hospital. He is a strong man now who has a responsible position with the Sears Roebuck Company, but his parents still carried with them, all these years since their emigration, a picture of Herta in her nurse's uniform. Unfortunately, the Silversteins were not well enough at the time to attend my party.

My other friend from school days, Erwin Zadik, was able to accept our invitation with his wife Ursula. He and I had also attended the lowest grades of Breslau's Koenig Wilhelms Gymnasium and lost track of each other completely. We had been about ten or eleven years old when we were in school together, and then—sixty years later—I read a short notice in *Aufbau* saying that Erwin Zadik had celebrated his seventieth birthday. It gave his address in the Bronx, and mentioned Breslau and Shanghai as his former whereabouts. There was no doubt in my mind who he was, and right away I sent him a congratulatory message, apologizing for the sixty-year "delay." The following Sunday he telephoned me, came down with his wife Ursula to my party, and we have been in contact ever since. People still cannot believe that we found each other after an interval of sixty years. Mel assured me that, in the United States, people who have gone to elementary school together often don't remember each other when they meet again after only twenty or thirty years. There must be a special bond between the survivors of the terrible twentieth-century tragedy. Erwin Zadik had also been an inmate of Buchenwald Concentration Camp, but I did not know that until 1983. There is a special bond. Even though Felix Taucher has passed away, Herta and I communicate regularly with his widow Dana, whom we have never met in person. She is a native-born American woman who lives in Joplin, Missouri.

Aside from these friends and my immediate family, there were a few relatives present at my special birthday party: Herta's sister Lucy, who had escaped Nazi Germany, her daughter, Ruth, granddaughter Sabrina, and great-grandson Marci. There was Mel's uncle Jack Raichelson, whose wife Ruth had been unable to make it. Also present was Mel's aunt, Rose Seidenberg, mother of Dr. Robert Seidenberg, a psychiatrist and friend of ours for many years. Our Michael was there in a wheelchair, accompanied by his home aide for the day, Ms. Barbara Lillis, and another aide at the time, Ms. Claire Bush. Also helping with Michael was Ralph Golio, a former tenant of ours on South Salina Street and now a maintenance man at Howard Johnsons in DeWitt. Needless to say, Eleene Seeber, who has been with Michael and us day and night for the past twenty-five years, was sitting next to our handicapped son—as was only to be expected. Mel was there, of course, and two of his school friends were there: Joe Jerry, an attorney who advises him in affairs of business, and his wife Madeline, and Al Small, who had introduced Joan to him. Al was a representative with the Billhuber-Knoll Pharmaceutical Company and was accompanied by his wife Shirley.

My cousins Eric and Inge Spitz had come down from Toronto to celebrate, and their cousin and friend of ours, Greta Lehmann from New York was also with us.

Sitting at the table with Dr. Baurice Laffer, the former police doctor, and his wife Helen were Dr. Dante Lombardi and his wife Rosa. We had met in California during the 1960s and have been good friends ever since. Not missing was our good friend, Rita Seligman. With her was her daughter Esther and grandson Kenny, a school friend of Sarah and Maurice. Rita was accompanied by Heinz Rothschild, whose parents were from Berlin.

Seated next to me were Congressman and Mrs. George Wortley. I had known the congressman since he was a boy working part-time in his father's drug store, the Tully Pharmacy. He was the first at the party to raise his glass and toast me.

I introduced the friends and relatives to each other and told them that I had not only received a nice birthday message from the House of Representatives but also a beautiful birthday card from President and Mrs. Reagan. Dr. Laffer, who had never received any kind of message from the White House, was very impressed. Whenever I had had my doubts about the economy or Social Security, Baurice always reassured me. Ronald Reagan could do no wrong, as far as my friend Baurice Laffer was concerned.

Everybody at the party took a few moments to congratulate me, then Congressman Wortley read to all of us the personal message from the President:

THE WHITE HOUSE
WASHINGTON

June 6, 1983

Dear Dr. Hartmann:

Nancy and I extend our wishes to you on your 70th birthday.

Over the years you have earned the deep admiration of your friends and patients you have served so well. I hope the fond memories of your life in America will brighten this occasion and will in some way eclipse those of the dreadful years you experienced during the war.

We are grateful that you chose to come to this country to continue your practice of medicine. You have given much to America.

God bless you.

Sincerely,
Ronald Reagan

Everybody was moved.

The closest I had come to politics before was in 1956 when I sent a letter to Dr. James Halsted, director of professional services at the Veterans Hospital in Syracuse, who was married to the daughter of President Franklin D. Roosesvelt, Anna Boettiger Roosevelt. I had complained about the lack of reports on my patients who were hospitalized at the local V.A. Hospital. In his reply to me, the physician signed the letter: "With kind regards, Sincerely yours, James A. Halsted."

The son-in-law of Franklin Delano Roosevelt had sent me "kind regards." But now I received a personal birthday message from the President of the United States. I had to get up and say something in response. This is what I told the audience:

> I thank the President of the United States for his beautiful birthday message. I don't really deserve it. There are other physicians who have done more or at least as much as I did. Yet, this letter was a good move on the part of the president—from now on I shall try to do much, much better.

I asked Congressman Wortley about the etiquette in a case like this. I knew the president would be too busy to read a thank-you note of mine. Mr. Wortley assured me he would take care of it for me as he was seeing President Reagan about twice a month.

Our little party didn't go unnoticed. Because of the congressman's presence and the presence of my two friends who had gone to school with me sixty years ago, the *Syracuse Sunday Herald* produced a picture of our group the next day. David Grunfeld, a graduate of the well-known Newhouse School of Communication at Syracuse University, was able to take our pictures. It so happens that his father, Walter Grunfeld, is the son of a Jewish cantor and teacher in Baden Baden, Germany, and is now the editor of several small town newspapers in Central New York.

The picture, with an explanatory text, was seen by many of my patients and friends, and I was flattered that many of them saved it and put it into frames at home. We all liked the little portrait, so I sent a note to the editor of the *Jewish Observer*, Mrs. Chayat, asking her to publish a copy of the picture. She not only agreed to that, but she also printed a nice interview with me. Later on, *Aufbau*, the little paper responsible for so many of the reunions that day, published a similar story.

Retirement

I have to go on with my medical practice again. Patients keep asking me, "When are you going to retire?" If I retired completely, I would not have my vacations to look forward to! It is not always easy to cut down on the patient load, with office rents going up and malpractice insurance rates increasing. At times, the physician gets disappointed and disillusioned when one of his patients ends up in the hospital emergency ward with an overdose of a prescribed tranquilizer or pain relief agent. Some are sick people in need of specialized treatment who tell you that they need these addictive drugs urgently as their "mother had just passed away," and they had to attend the funeral. Soon enough you find out that their mother is living and in perfect physical condition. Some physicians in various specialties might never have the need to prescribe controlled substances in their practices. Some even advise other doctors not to use any of those substances in treating patients. I think that is a "copout." There is still the need in medicine for the relief of real pain and for the treatment of anxiety disorders or grief situations. The addicts, on the other hand, are sick people who need supervision to get away from those dangerous drugs in order to protect themselves and others. I am unable to comprehend those experts who would like to see the sale of controlled substances legalized, without the need for prescriptions. They claim that in free America each person should have the choice of whether to take the drugs or leave them alone. Unfortunately, not everybody is intelligent or has insight enough to see the complications and dangers of drug abuse.

The same experts don't see any need for generalists, internists, or psychiatrists to interfere with the plans of suicidal patients. Again, they claim that if the person wants to commit suicide, the person should be allowed to do it in this free country. Yet, so many suicide victims who have been saved express their gratitude; they come to realize that they had been suffering from a lack of judgment while under the influence of their depression.

Look at the New York State seat belt law! Numbers of people contend that they have heard about accidents in which the driver would have been killed had he worn a seat belt. But, the majority admit that seat belts may protect the lives of thousands of people every year. Many of those people say that drivers should take educational courses but should never be forced to wear seat belts by government rule. You know by now that this writer came from a totalitarian country, from Nazi Germany. I wish that the seat belt law would have been their most restrictive law! No need to tell you that no such law was in effect there.

In spite of the fact that I have cut down on my patient load, I have not given up my Medicaid patients. My old surgical group of Drs. Sarason, Burdick, Nathan, and Mendel never fail to see any of those people in need, and Dr. Irving Goldman, the urologist, has never turned them down. Dr. Reinhard Bothe, orthopedic surgeon, has always accepted them. My own dentist, Dr. Henry Cramer, brother-in-law of the late beloved pediatrician, Dr. Robert Schwartz, gladly takes care of Medicaid patients' dental problems. I can very well understand all those specialists who feel unable to accept the low payments from Social Services, as these doctors have such a high overhead with their large staffs and increasingly exorbitant malpractice insurance rates. There was once a study undertaken by some psychologists who had been hired by organizations critical of the Medicaid system. They "found" that most of the physicians who accept Medicaid patients have not had good training, attend hardly any postgraduate courses, and spend very little time with their patients. Their statement did not make me think less of Medicaid doctors, but it made me wonder about certain psychologists.

My accountant for decades had been Sidney Josef, originally from Stuttgart, I believe; and, since his retirement with his wife to Arizona, his former associate Arnold Hodes has been preparing my taxes for me. I am writing this because with the freezing of doctors' fees by Medicare, voluntary fee freezes, and the ever-increasing malpractice insurance, even younger physicians have to decide whether it is worthwhile to stay on in private practice. These were the concerns of Dr. Joseph F. Boyle, an internist from Los Angeles and president of the American Medical Association, who spoke at the Medical Grand Rounds in Syracuse recently. He told us about the efforts of the A.M.A. to outlaw boxing, the only sport in which it is mandatory to injure the opponent. He mentioned the fight promoters' criticisms of the doctors, who accuse them of ulterior motives. Sometimes, it seems that the majority of the population does not think very highly of physicians in general. They are not very caring, they say; they show no compassion, don't spend enough time with their patients, and charge exhorbitant fees. All the persons questioned, though, were able to point out one exception—their own doctor.

People are worried about Michael's and my own future. My own plans are intertwined with those of my family and Michael's. "What will you do?" they ask. "Everybody is mortal; nobody lives forever." I cannot answer them to their satisfaction. I did not see the coming of Nazi Germany; I did not anticipate Michael's disability or Herta's illnesses. There is an old German proverb (again), *"Dier Mensch denkt, und Gott lenkt"* (Man thinks, and God directs). All we fallible humans can do is try to do the right thing. The rest is not up to us.

My doctor friends and myself try to keep Michael out of hospitals, if at all possible. If illness strikes, home is the best place for him. If he is really sick, feverish, nauseated, or has stomach cramps, he calls "Dad." He trusts me completely; I don't have to produce my medical license each time.

When we attended the first meetings of the Association for Retarded Children about thirty years ago, we were given advice by experts and estate lawyers on how to build trust funds or other funds to guarantee a life-income for our disabled children. The more lectures we heard, the more scared we became. There are not any millionaries among us, and it seems that nobody could be able to afford those high premiums for meaningful insurance.

Michael is now on Social Security, Medicaid, and extended Blue Cross and Blue Shield. We are lucky that Joan, Mel, and the grandchildren live so close and that they are always there when needed. They cannot do enough for Michael. The fact that society helps to take care of the handicapped is a sign of an advanced civilization. These social programs are the best we have, although there is much to be desired. It is obvious that even high-income families can go broke if one of their members suddenly comes down with a cruel, incurable disease. It is up to us to elect public representatives to work with us for a broader social legislation.

It is no hardship for parents to bring up these special children if there is love and affection at home. Who does not remember the motto on Boys' Town stationery, "He ain't heavy, Father, he is my brother"? I just read recently the story of David Rabin, a world-famous doctor and specialist in endocrinology, who suffered from A.L.S., or Lou Gehrig's disease. The beautiful book, titled *Six Parts of Love* and written by his daughter Roni, describes the physician's difficulties in breathing, disturbance of swallowing, and isolation from friends who did not know how to behave in a case like that—but always the family's love came shining through. It is a heart-warming book; one would expect to find it on the best seller list. I purchased the book, which occupies an honored place in my library.

It was in May 1984 that I became a life member of and received a gold pin from the Onondaga County Medical Society. The award dinner was held at the Lafayette Country Club. Any doctor above the age of seventy becomes a life member now, and I received my pin with Drs. Hamel, Menter, Amodio, and Piirak from the then president, Dr. Edward Hughes. Strangely enough, it was my wife Herta who had contacted several society presidents over the years (the doctors Tilley, Konys, and Stewart), until the decision was made to honor the older physicians. According to an article by Gerald N. Hoffman, executive director of the Society, in the Medical Society's *Bulletin,* it was Dr. Carl Marlow who suggested the pin and Mrs. Olga LaTessa, wife of ophthalmologist Dr. Anthony LaTessa, who helped to design them.

Sitting with us at our table were Mel and Joan, as well as Dr. Edward Piirak, a graduate of the University of Tartu in Estonia. Another table companion was Dr. Zigurds Suritis, a well-known plastic surgeon, with his wife, a former nurse. He is associated in his practice with Dr. David Stark. Next to Dr. Suritis were seated Dr. and Mrs. Arthur Lehrman, another distinguished plastic surgeon on the teaching staff of Syracuse's Medical College. Dr. and Mrs. Lehrman are seasoned travelers. In 1979 he took part in the Care-Medico Program to teach residents of Afghanistan working at three hospitals to perform surgery under the most primitive conditions. While in Afghanistan, he visited the Jewish community of Kabul. I saw him that year with Rabbi Irwin Hyman on "Jewish Journal," a local television show, where he reported about his interesting trip. I myself did not go so far to find communities of "exotic" Jews, but, about forty-five years ago, when I was preparing for my medical state board, I went to the Bronx to attend services at a black synagogue. The people of that congregation were praying and singing in Hebrew, the rabbi spoke in English, and I was able to follow the service as well as in any other synagogue. These Jewish families had fled from Ethiopia after Mussolini had invaded their country.

Associated with Dr. Lehrman is another renowned plastic surgeon, Dr. Alfred Falcone. In 1980 he and his wife were honored by the Syracuse Right to Life Foundation, because they are "so pro family life." The Falcones have eight children, four biological and four adopted. Among those eight are also two "special children." Dr. Falcone is a former president of the Syracuse Chapter of the Association for Retarded Children.

I recently attended one of these medical dinner-lecture meetings at one of the city's finest restaurants. It was sponsored, as is so often the case, by Merck, Sharp and Dohme, editors of the internationally known *Merck Manual.* A professor from Pittsburgh was the speaker, and he talked about arrhythmias. I have found all the medical companies most helpful to our profession, and these dinner meetings enable us to meet and exchange ideas with other doctors in a relaxed atmosphere. I was accompanied to this dinner meeting by Dr. Laffer, and across from the table sat Dr. Armand Cincotta of Liverpool, New York. Dr. Cincotta, who is in family practice, told us about his four children: His oldest daughter attends Tufts Medical School in Boston, and his youngest boy, age fourteen, is a "special child." He is proud of all of them.

The next day, when visiting the Grand Rounds at Upstate Medical Center, I saw Dr. Edward Schoenheit, an internist who had left active medical practice and went into law school. I understand that he passed his law examinations. In recent years many doctors have earned degrees in both fields. Maybe the high awards in so-called malpractice cases, with higher and higher insurance premiums that force many physicians out of practice, have awakened an interest in those doctors in the study of law. They all keep up, though, with their medical education.

My friend Dr. Julius Krombach, now 84 years old and retired in Florida, wrote a most interesting letter to the prestigious *New York State Journal of Medicine,* outlining his thoughts about AIDS disease. He received many requests for reprints, at least two of them from Berlin. In June of 1984 he published in the same medical journal a much-discussed article called "A Foreign Physician in Russia in the 1930s." He had been sent there as a refugee from Hitler Germany by the American Joint Distribution Committee until he and his little family were finally able to sail to the United States.

On a visit to my doctor, Murray Grossman, he mentioned to me that Audio Digest of California, which edits audiocassettes for thousands of physicians, had taped a lecture he had given in November of 1983 at an Upstate Medical Center postgraduate course in Sarasota, Florida. I got the tape. His lecture is titled

"Puzzling Types of Chest Pains," and on the reverse side (what an honor!) is the classic 1962 lecture by Dr. Walter C. Alvarez, one of the late giants of medicine, about "Puzzling Types of Abdominal Pain" that he had given before the American Medical Association.

All these medical encounters make it impossible for the physician to forget his profession—whether he is retired, semi-retired, or in active medical practice. Just remembering the medical history of my family makes me also remember the time given so freely by our doctor friends: Dr. Mark Harwood, orthopedic surgeon, who aspirated Michael's knee after an injury; Drs. Eric Pettit and Lester Steinholz, who did some difficult dental extractions; Dr. Harry Levitt, dermatologist, who treated some of Herta's skin lesions; and many, many others. And then, in August 1984, I found a small notice in *Aufbau* by a Dr. Eric Kohler, associate professor of history at the University of Wyoming. He asked to be contacted for a research project concerning the "immigration of Jewish physicians to the U.S. during the 1930s and early 1940s." We corresponded many times, and that gave me a chance to recollect many things I had almost forgotten.

At one point, Dr. Kohler needed answers to so many questions that he suggested I use an audio cassette. I did give my answers on tape and was promised an abstract of my recording. I received a faithful transcript of my tape before the end of 1984, and Professor Kohler told me an amusing story in this connection. The typist, a native of Tennessee, had transcribed some interviews with "local oldtimers" at the beginning of her secretarial career for the University of Wyoming. She felt a little apprehensive when she was told by Dr. Kohler that she would "encounter a German accent" when listening to my tape. After completing the transcript of my cassette, she explained to the professor, "Your doctor is much easier to understand than the locals were!"

There was one important question I was not able to answer from my own experience. Professor Kohler wanted to hear about the differences between the medical practice in the Germany of pre-Hitler days and practice in the United States of America. I never did get a chance to go into private practice in Germany.

Dr. Kohler has been interviewing physicians much older than I, and their close relatives.

He visited me once, the summer of 1985, in Syracuse. In May 1985, Professor Kohler presented his preliminary findings on these immigrant physicians to the American Association for the History of Medicine. The meeting was held in Durham, North Carolina, and his paper, *Some Preliminary Findings on German Jewish Physicians in America, 1933-1955,* evoked a lot of interest among his listeners. I am looking very much forward to seeing his finished research project.

We are all addicted to our profession, not a bad addiction. Here's a little story to show what I mean: Many years ago in Syracuse I asked Dr. John Ayer, an internist whose late father, Dr. Wardner Ayer, had been a professor of medicine here, to see a patient of mine in consultation. When I apologized for the lateness of my call, Dr. Ayer replied, "There is nothing better than to be called away from a dull party."

Visits

Because of Herta's various medical problems, especially her herniated disk disease, we have recently been unable to go for a short vacation to the Concord or similar Catskill resorts or to attend any of the festivities we have been invited to. In 1984, we did not have any relatives from California visit, but once every weekend Herta phoned her sister Lucy or one of her nieces; it is the only luxury she has. It was a pleasant surprise for us when Henry and Ilse Mertens from White Plains came with their young journalist daughter Evelyn to our house before the end of 1984. They attended a large Bristol Laboratories meeting here. We had been friends when Henry had had an important position with the local plant. For the past two or three decades, he has been working at the executive offices of Bristol Myers Company in New York City. We never lost track of each other, and we were very happy to see them again in Syracuse.

In September of 1984 we were invited to a Bat Mitzvah in Toronto, but Herta did not feel quite able to travel and participate in the festivities. Sheri Anne, the Bat Mitzvah girl, is the granddaughter of Uschi Miller, who with her brother Eric Spitz had undertaken the nightmarish journey on the notorious *St. Louis*. They all felt bad that for the first time in many years it was not possible for us to attend one of their joyous celebrations. So, on one of the last Sundays of 1984, the whole family came to Syracuse from Canada to spend several hours with us: Uschi and her husband Johnny, their daughter Judy with her husband, Dr. Arnie Katz, who is medical director of a large company, and their five children. Aside from other beautiful gifts, they brought along a nicely framed collection of pictures of Sheri Anne's special day. They also played the video tape of her Bat Mitzvah, and, in return, we played the video cassette of my seventieth birthday celebration, which they had missed. A wonderful, memorable occasion!

A few weeks later, we were visited by our other cousins, Eric and Inge Spitz from Toronto, and Grete Lehmann, our common friend from New York. Inge and Eric are able to come to our city twice a year as their three sons are grown up and married now. On this latest trip they stayed over the weekend and brought along some worthwhile gifts that were really not necessary, yet deeply appreciated. It was marvelous to listen to "Pavarotti's Greatest Hits" on the two cassettes they brought me, but it was the other tape they had brought along that really started me thinking.

The second tape is called *"Noten, die verboten wurden"* (Notes, that were forbidden), a recording of music that the Third Reich had banned. Recently, a paperback edition of Bernt Engelmann's *Germany Without Jews* came out, translated from the original German hardcover edition. In the book, Engelmann retails the historical fact that under the Nazi regime all the musicians of Jewish descent had to leave the country and that German artists were not permitted to perform the works of Jewish composers of international fame. Not only were great conductors like Bruno Walter and Otto Klemperer banned from Germany, but non-Jewish conductors were not allowed to play the music of Mendelssohn, Meyerbeer, Offenbach, or Mahler, to name just a few. *"Noten, die verboten wurden,"* though, plays mostly the melodies of the Jewish operetta composers Emmerich Kalman, Leo Fall, and Paul Abraham. As I have mentioned before, the German government pays restitution claims to former victims of the Nazi persecution; in addition, some of the larger cities like Berlin, Hamburg, and Munich invite those elderly people as guests to their old hometowns. I remember vividly that composer Paul Abraham, who was able to escape from Nazi Germany, became emotionally ill and had to spend years in American psychiatric institutions. The German post-war government called him back and paid for his care in a psychiatric hospital. He was released and was still able to conduct his own compositions for a while. It was a great event one New Year's night when a performance of Paul Abraham's "Blume von Hawaii" was held at Breslau's Stadt Theater. But, sadly enough, the composer fell back into his diseased state of mind and died in the country of his birth.

It is surprising to hear on *Noten, die verboten wurden* the melodies of Irving Berlin, the American composer of "White Christmas," "Easter Parade," and (last, but not least) "God Bless America." As a Jew he was banned in Nazi Germany.

In March, 1986, I saw my friend Franz Josef Nave for the first time since we were classmates in Breslau's Koenig Wilhelms Gymnasium. It was his father who had been asked to retire early from his job as a judge by the German government because of his political disagreement with Hitler's government. In 1952 or 1953, Franz Josef, a non-Jew, came to the United States to continue his pediatric training here. He is now a retired pediatrician living in Cincinnati. He has three sons, but he lost his wife recently; she had suffered from rheumatoid arthritis for many years.

Since I found out several years ago that Franz Josef was in this country, we have been corresponding and speaking over the phone with each other. His visit was very important to me, and it was also considered a newsworthy event by the *Sunday Herald,* which, thanks to staff writer Bob Curley and photographer David Lassman, put our pictures in the paper.

There was never a lull in our conversation as we remembered together the common friends and acquaintances, Jews or non-Jews, who had touched our lives. Dr. Nave was a friend of Professor Leichtentritt, a former professor of pediatrics in Breslau. He'd also had to leave Germany because of his Jewish descent. Franz Josef and I both agreed that medicine is almost the only profession that allows a person to do some good, even in a dictatorship. He was familiar with the statement of the German psychiatrist Ernst Kretschmer who, referring to Hitler after the collapse of the Nazis, said, "In good times we certify them [send them to mental hospitals], and in bad times they rule over us."

The first time Franz Josef went into Michael's room, he smiled at Michael, and Michael smiled right back. Michael even made some movement with his hand, indicating that he wanted Franz Josef to come back again. In the short time that Franz Josef was practicing medicine before he came to the United States, he observed two children who became brain damaged after receiving the prophylactic whooping cough vaccine.

For decades I have always been ready to see salesmen or representatives of pharmaceutical houses. They supplied me with literature about their newest products, answered questions I might have, left starter supplies for private patients who were not rich, and finally made sure that I received large amounts of physicians' clinical supplies whenever a family member needed them urgently. I shall enumerate just a few of these companies that come to mind right now: Abbott; Ayerst; Ciba; Lilly and Dista; Boehringer-Ingelheim; Upjohn; Bristol; Pfizer; Merck; Sharp and Dohme; Robbins; Roche; Hoechst; Merrell-Dow; Squibb; Glaxo; Schering; Smith, Kline, and French; Billhuber-Knoll; Massengill; Parke-Davis; Stuart; Syntex; Mead-Johnson; Wyeth; Wallace; Winthrop; Marion; Searle; Lederle; Beecham Laboratories; Pennwalt; Roerig; Sandoz; Purdue-Frederick; McNeil; Riker; Endo; Dorsey; Flint; Burroughs Wellcome Company. I ask forgiveness if I slighted anybody. Some have been calling me for decades, and lately I mentioned this autobiographical book to a few. I was asked in jest by Paul Barkal of the Schering Company, "Will you write about me?" I had to decline, explaining that impossible it was to single anybody out among the many, many representatives who call on me. "Then at least write about us detailmen and what we do," he replied.

Now I have to mention Mr. Barkal's name because of a most recent tragic event. I met him at Birnbaum's Funeral Parlor, where he also paid his last respects to our good friend Alan Small, who had suddenly passed away at the age of forty-five. There has been no death in recent years that has shocked me and so many others to such an extent. About two days later, our cousin Inge's younger sister Edith died, due to a malignant disease. Eight years ago, we lost Dr. Kenneth Ruppel, a pediatrician friend, unexpectedly. He also had been of great help whenever his services were needed for our Michael. In all these cases we had to ask why it happened to their families, and why it happened to us. Both Rabbi Sherman and Rabbi Irwin Hyman pointed out in their moving eulogies for Al that we have many more questions than answers. Al was a man who was, not only very young and in generally good health, but also full of life, always ready to help others—visiting the lonely in the hospital, giving assurance to the discouraged. He is survived by his wife Shirley and his two children, Steven and Barbara. Barbara, age 15, spoke to the capacity crowd at the funeral parlor about her feelings.

Al Small had attended Syracuse University and knew Joan and Mel since college days. It was he who introduced them. We had been living on the same street with Al Small and his family for a long time. Whenever I went away with my own family for a short vacation, Al, like Rita Seligman and the Irving Cantors, checked on Michael, who still was watched over by Eleene every single day. After college he went into the pharmaceutical field.

Al's first job as a representative was with the Armour Company. When Armour changed hands, he became sales representative for Billhuber-Knoll, a pharmaceutical outfit I had been familiar with since my European days. Like some of the other well-known companies, Knoll arranged for professional dinner-meetings with local or out of town medical speakers, and Al was in charge of these social gatherings. The first one took place at Syracuse's LeMoyne Manor, and Dr. Daniel S. Fuleihan, a local cardiologist, was the speaker. I talked with Al for the very last time at one of these dinner meetings at which he introduced Dr. Bruce Marmor, another cardiologist of this city, who gave a fine talk about the problem of angina. This dinner meeting was a memorable one for still another reason. I had gone with my good friend, Dr. Baurice Laffer, to Pascale's Restaurant. Across the dinner table from us sat two charming ladies, Miss Sandra Lemberger, a senior medical student at Dr. Marmor's office whose grandparents survived a Nazi concentration camp, and Ms. Anne Clancy, a nurse at Dr. Marmor's office, of Catholic background. We had a most interesting conversation, and both encouraged me to write my book. I was told that even Dr. Marmor wanted to see my autobiography in print. All that made me feel good, but I still don't or can't believe that Al Small is gone.

On Writing

Writing this book has been a wonderful experience for me. By the end of 1984 I had been writing for about two years, but I was still somehow addicted to my autobiographical story. If ever a day went by that I didn't work on my story, I felt blue indeed. I could make as much progress writing on days when I was working as I could on days when I was on vacation.

I was most anxious to make an agreement with a publishing company I liked and admired, as was the case with Prometheus. But, in the meantime, I wanted to be sure my labor was not lost; I would like my book to be read by as many people as possible—friends, patients, and strangers. Soon after I finished my original manuscript, I sent a copy of it to the Leo Baeck Institute in New York City so that it could be used by their visiting scholars. This research organization, which has branch offices in London and Jerusalem, has saved in their archives documents, pictures, and memoirs pertaining to the history of German Jewry. They sent me a beautiful thank-you note for leaving a copy of my manuscript with them, and I was most grateful for their acknowledgement.

As my writing progressed, I was always curious about what the next chapter would bring. Many people came back to life for me. Others I didn't mention have surely meant as much to me and might have influenced me more. Dr. Donald Woolfolk was one of the internists who treated Michael when he had to be hospitalized; the doctor has since moved with his family to North Carolina. Mrs. Regina Schmidt, one of our old tenants from South Salina Street, lives now in Germany but, at age 84, visits her daughter Desiree in California every year. Then we are able to talk to her over the phone. Gracyna Widman, who studied special education at Syracuse University with my daughter Joan, now lives with her husband Vic and their two children near Albany, New York.

I also made some new friends in the process of writing my book. When I began to correspond with Dr. Ronald Pies, he was professor of psychiatry at Penn State University. Since that time he has written a book of poems called *Lean Soil;* he often writes letters to the editor to the *New York Times* or other big newspapers; and there are articles by him in American and British medical journals. He is now an associate director of the acute care unit at Tufts Mental Health Center and an assistant professor of psychiatry at Tufts University. Still, he finds time to answer my letters and inquiries.

It was in 1982 when I decided to write my autobiographical story, but I had to postpone it from one month to another because, whenever a new book came out that in some way dealt with my life history, I had to read it first. As I didn't have time to sit and read in libraries, I had to purchase these volumes before they got out of print. My personal library got bigger and bigger. For years I made it a habit not to lend books to anyone—I never knew if they would be returned to me in time if I should really need them.

I also re-read articles. "Bearing Witness" by Samuel G. Freedman, which appeared in the *New York Times Magazine,* is about the life and work of Elie Wiesel. Now a professor of humanities at Boston University, Wiesel is a survivor of Buchenwald Concentration Camp, where his parents and youngest sister perished. He started to write about the Holocaust ten years after the tragic event, and he has never stopped. The introduction to his first novel, *Night,* was written by Francois Mauriac, the French Nobel laureate. When Wiesel was interviewing the devoutly Catholic Mauriac, "He was talking about Christ, and I simply said to him, 'Ten years ago I knew hundreds of Jewish children who suffered more than Christ did and no one talks about it.' And he wept. He said, 'You know, you should talk about it.' And that moved me more than anything." That same day he started to write *Night.*

Elie Wiesel spoke a short time ago at Syracuse's Hendricks Chapel for a very large audience. But, in general, many people in the United States are "sick and tired" of hearing about the Holocaust. This tragic event seems too incomprehensible to be believable. Strangely enough, the younger generation in Germany is trying to come to grips with the fate of the Jewish citizens of their country under the Nazi regime. Not too many years go, there appeared in the *Jerusalem Post* a letter by an M. B. Dessaur who said that he still felt some hate in his heart for the German people because of everything that had happened. Somehow, his letter found its way into a high school class in Germany, and twenty-five pupils sent their responses to Mr. Dessaur. A large correspondence developed that is still in existence today. Many of these German boys and girls visited Israel, and many elderly Jews paid a visit to their high school. The whole correspondence has been published in Germany under the title *Briefe an junge Deutsche* (Letters to young Germans).

Another article I re-read for my book was an interview of Roman Vishniac by Herbert Mitgang for the *New York Times Magazine*. Vishniac, the world-famous photographer, grew up and earned an M.D. degree in Moscow and immigrated to Berlin with his family after the Russian Revolution. As a Jew, he had always been interested in his ancestry, so he took pictures in Germany and all over Europe—wherever his fellow Jews were endangered or deported—in order to record the vanishing world of the Jews in Europe and to alert the rest of the world about what was happening. He had been able to handle a camera since he was seven years old, but taking pictures in Nazi Germany took more than skill with a camera—it also took imagination and courage.

Dr. Vishniac took about 160,000 photographs between 1934 and 1939 but was able to get only 2,000 of them out of the country. The first pictures he took in 1934 were of large Nazi signs on a Berlin store. To do this, he disguised himself in a Nazi uniform and posed his daughter in front of the store so that, when a policeman asked him what he was up to, he was able to answer that he was taking pictures of his daughter. Once he photographed stormtroopers burning books in front of the Reichstrag during *Kristlnacht*.

By 1938 it was quite a bit harder for Roman Vishniac to take the photographs he needed, even with his hidden camera. The S.S. had deported ten thousand Polish Jews living in Germany to a filthy barracks in a Polish border town. The conditions there were so terrible that many of the people died of pneumonia. The American representative to the League of Nations demanded that something be done about it, but the Polish ambassador, a Nazi collaborator, labeled the report about the barbarism a "Jewish fabrication." Dr. Vishniac wanted to get photographic documentation of what was really going on, and he knew he had to act quickly. It was easy for him, and his hidden camera, to get into the camp; he joined a group of new arrivals. But it wasn't so easy to leave the camp again, in spite of the fact that, in 1938, the security measures at the camp were not as perfect as they would be in later years. After two unsuccessful attempts, Vishniac finally escaped by jumping from the second floor of the barracks at night. According to the photographer, "When my photographs arrived in Geneva, the Polish representative reportedly shouted, 'Who took these pictures?' I'm sorry I wasn't there to tell him that I did."

In 1939, he succeeded in getting to France, and in 1941 he arrived in New York with a small fraction of his negatives sewn into his clothing. *A Vanished World* by Roman Vishniac is full of pictures of wonderful, learned, and saintly people who "disappeared" simply because they were Jews.

At the end of the *Times* interview, Dr. Vishniac handed Herbert Mitgang an excerpt from an 1891 essay by Leo Tolstoy called "What is a Jew?":

> The Jew is a holy being who brought the eternal fire from heaven that illuminated the earth and all living on it. He is the source and the well from which all other nations have drawn their religion and beliefs. . . . The Jew is the discoverer of freedom. . . . The Jew is a symbol of civic and religious tolerance. . . . The Jew is a symbol of eternity.

The millions of Jewish men, women, and children who perished during the Holocaust fit Tolstoy's description exactly.

The stories of these people and many others inspired me to write my own life's story, and the writing itself has become an important part of my life. It is this book that has united me with human beings I have never met, big minds and smaller minds, past and present.

. . . Always a Doctor

A doctor cannot retire from medicine, even if he wants to. In 1968 an anthology was published by Little, Brown and Company under the title *Familiar Medical Quotations,* by Maurice B. Strauss, M.D. At the request of the editor, many doctors including myself sent in some quotes which we had missed in that original edition. Fred Belleveau, general manager of the Medical Division, thanked me for my quotation and promised to save it for the next edition. I first saw it in a newspaper column by the late showman Billy Rose; I saved it, and here it is again:

> For my dough, the most important people in the world are doctors. If you cut yourself, if something starts biting at your insides, if your kid breaks out in spots, whom do you holler for? Your Congressman? The president of your bank? The secretary of War? Not on your tintype. You send for the man with the little black satchel. . . .
> When I was a kid, I had scarlet fever, and they tacked a sign on my house and nobody could come near me. But a small gent with a black bag walked right in. . . .
> I remember asking my mother, "Can't doctors catch scarlet fever?" She said they couldn't—but she was fibbing. The list of doctors who were killed by the bugs they were chasing would stretch from here to Valhalla. Of course the great standouts of medical science don't need any ballyhoo from me. But the doctor who rides around in that 1947 Chevy could use a little applause. In a civilization that rates a guy by how a big check he can write, the doctor knocks his brains out for less than we pay a bricklayer

or a plumber. Sun or slush, he is on tap if you're in trouble. Twenty-four hours a day he stands ready to stop what's hurting you. To me that's as important as anybody can get.

Some readers might take issue with Billy Rose's piece of journalism. They claim that their doctor does not drive around in a 1947 Chevy. Of course not. One shouldn't forget, either, that Billy Rose wrote that column decades ago. And do they really want their doctor to run around in an old beaten up car to make hospital and home calls? "My doctor doesn't make any home calls," they reply. But, please consider that more efficient prescriptions can be given over the phone, and better equipment and services are available at the physician's office than at the patient's home. And, who would argue today for a home visit in case of a heart attack or myocardial infarction, for which the stricken person should be transferred to a hospital emergency ward right away?

Much more well-known is a quotation of Robert Louis Stevenson, the British novelist and poet who lived in the second half of the nineteenth century. This one is quoted in *Familiar Medical Quotations* as well as in A. C. Corcoran's *A Mirror Up To Medicine* and other medical anthologies. It goes like this:

> There are men and classes of men that stand above the common herd; the soldier, the sailor, and the shepherd not infrequently; the artist rarely; rarelier still, the clergyman; the physician almost as a rule. He is the flower (such as it is) of our civilization. Generosity he has, such as is possible only to those who practice an art, never to those who drive a trade; discretion, tested by a hundred secrets; tact tried in a thousand embarrassments; and what are more important, Herculean cheerfulness and courage.

But, it is not so much approval or praise that the physician asks for. He wants to be able to live with himself, and to do the best he can in his chosen profession as Healer. For centuries, physicians have been following the Hippocratic Oath or similar guidelines. Being of Jewish heritage, I shall recite here the "Oath of Maimonides." In front of me is a framed copy of that oath, given to me by Syracuse's Bristol Laboratories. Maimonides was born in Cordoba in the year 1135 and practiced last in Cairo, Egypt, where he died in 1208. He was not only a great physician but also a distinguished philosopher who reconciled the philosophy of Aristotle with Judaism. His Physician's Oath can be followed without pangs of conscience by fundamentalists and people of all religions as well as by secular humanists, and here is the Oath of Maimonides:

> Thy eternal providence has appointed me to watch over life and health of Thy creatures.
> May the love for my art actuate me at all times; may neither avarice nor miserliness, nor thirst for glory, or for a great reputation engage my mind; for the enemies of truth and philanthropy could easily deceive me and make me forgetful of my lofty aim of doing good to Thy children. May I never see in the patient anything but a fellow creature in pain. Grant me strength, time, and opportunity always to correct what I have acquired, always to extend its domain; for knowledge is immense and the spirit of man can extend infinitely to enrich itself daily with new requirements. Today he can discover his errors of yesterday and tomorrow he may obtain a new light on what he thinks himself sure of today.
> O, God, Thou hast appointed me to watch over the life and death of Thy creatures; here am I ready for my vocation, and now I turn into my calling.

Having finished my book, I shall try to concentrate on this medical task.

Afterword

Before I finish this book, I feel that I have to defend myself against some criticisms by my own family. "You write so much about other people, even books," they say, "and not enough about yourself." I find this remark most flattering but not quite true. I wrote much about myself, I know; I am not overly humble. I have even been vain enough to ask George Benedict, art teacher at the Jamesville/DeWitt High Schools, to paint a family picture of us. On top of that, I look into the mirror every day. I shall tell you why. On an ordinary day during office hours, my patients give me completely different versions of my own health. "How dapper you look," one might say; "You look a little tired today," is the opinion of another. "What do you do to stay so young?" one quips; "Age is creeping up on you," another one remarks. "I wish I could keep my weight down like you do," somebody tells me; "Eating seems to agree with you," a patient scolds me; "You have put on a few pounds," I hear from somebody else. Patients are not good judges of your health. You might become a hypochondriac if you listen to them too much. Luckily, the mirror helps out.

All the people I wrote about have meant something to me, and there are countless others I did not mention who mean as much to me. Our lives are intertwined with the lives of other people, or as Dr. Wilder Penfield titled his autobiography, *No Man Alone.*

This brings to mind also the saying of Rabbi Hillel, who was born in the first century before the common era and was noted for his humility and wisdom:

> If I am not for myself, who is for me?
> And if I am only for myself, what am I?
> And if not now, when?

I shall conclude with another story about Hillel, quoted so often that I am a little afraid to repeat it again, but many of my readers might never have heard of this sage, and I don't know of anything better to leave them with:

> A heathen once came before the sage Shammai [a very strict teacher]. He said to him, "I will convert to Judaism if you will teach me all the Torah while I stand on one foot."
> Shammai pushed the man away with the builder's measure he held in his hand. The man came before Hillel and repeated his request.
> Hillel said to him, "What is hateful to you do not do to your neighbor. That is the whole Torah. The rest is commentary—go and learn it."

I cannot improve on that story. But, please let me thank some of the people who helped me with this book:

I wish to thank very much Professor Paul Kurtz, editor in chief of Prometheus Books, who, in spite of a very busy schedule, encouraged me from the start and answered all my questions.

My thanks go also to Doris Doyle, director of the Trade Division at Prometheus, who assigned Elizabeth Rosch to be copy editor of my manuscript. It has been a most pleasant experience for me to work with this fine young lady to reach our common goal of making my book as readable as possible.

My appreciation also goes to Nancy Kosow, Executive Secretary of the Jewish Community Center in Syracuse, who professionally retyped a large part of my manuscript when I needed her services urgently.

I also want to express my appreciation to Professor Eric Kohler, the only person outside my family to whom I gave my manuscript to read. He was kind enough to give me suggestions and ideas.

Last, but not least, I thank my family for putting up with my strange hours of writing, in addition to my usual medical duties.

Having a pretty good memory myself, I was surprised that Herta remembered many events that I had almost forgotten. Joan and Mel were always there for criticism and encouragement.

I hope that my readers will get as much enjoyment from reading my book as I did from writing it.

> I am not a poet, as you can see,
> But just an ordinary M.D.
> Best wishes to Buddhists, Christians, and Jews.
> To all, from Heinz Hartmann in Syracuse.

Recommended Reading

American Jews in Community Crisis, Gerald S. Strober. Garden City, N.Y.: Doubleday, 1974.
The Autobiography of Wilhelm Stekel, Wilhelm Stekel. New York, N.Y.: Liveright, 1950.
Edith Stein, expanded edition, Waltrand Herbstrith. New York, N.Y.: Harper and Row, 1983.
Encyclopedia Judaica, 16 volumes. Jerusalem: Keter and New York, N.Y: Macmillan, 1972. (Decennial Volume, 1982).
Flim-Flam!, James Randi. Buffalo, N.Y.: Prometheus Books, 1982.
From a Minyan to a Community, B. G. Rudolph. Syracuse, N.Y.: Syracuse University Press, 1974.
Generation Without Memory, Anne Roiphe. New York, N.Y.: Linden Press, 1982.
The Healing Heart, Norman Cousins. New York, N.Y.: Norton, 1983.
In the Hell of Auschwitz, Judith Sternberg Newman. Smithtown, N.Y.: Exposition Press, 1978.
The Jewish People in Christian Preaching, ed. by Darrell Fasching. Lewiston, N.Y.: The Edwin Mellen Press, 1984.
Jews and Christians After the Holocaust, ed. by Abraham J. Peck. Philadelphia, Penn.: Fortress Press, 1982.
Man's Search for Meaning, Viktor Frankl. New York, N.Y.: Washington Square Press, 1963.
Martin Buber's Life and Work, 3 volumes. Maurice Friedman, New York, N.Y.: Dutton, 1983.

The Myth of Mental Illness, Thomas Szasz. New York, N.Y.: Harper and Row, 1974.
Night, Elie Wiesel. New York, N.Y.: Pyramid Books, 1961.
No Man Alone, Wilder Penfield. Boston, Mass.: Little Brown, 1977.
An Orphan in History, Paul Cowan. Garden City, N.Y.: Doubleday, 1982.
The Parnas, Silvano Arieti. New York, N.Y.: Basic Books, 1979.
Six Parts of Love, Roni Rabin. New York, N.Y.: Scribners, 1985.
Strangers in Their Own Land, Peter Sichrovsky. New York, N.Y.: Basic Books, 1986.
The Survivor in Us All, Erna Rubenstein. Hamden, Conn.: Archon Books, 1983.
The Therapeutic State, Thomas Szasz. Buffalo, N.Y.: Prometheus Books, 1984.
Thomas Szasz: Primary Values and Major Contentions, Richard Vatz and Lee Weinberg. Buffalo, N.Y.: Prometheus Books, 1983.
A Time to Remember, Marie Jastrow. New York, N.Y.: Norton, 1979.
A Vanished World, Roman Vishniac. New York, N.Y.: Farrar, Strauss, and Giroux, 1983.
The Victim's Song, Alice Kaminsky. Buffalo, N.Y.: Prometheus Books, 1985.
Voyage of the Damned, Gordon Thomas and Max Morgan-Witts. Briarcliff Manor, N.Y.: Stein and Day, 1974.
Voices of Wisdom, Francine Klagbrun. New York, N.Y.: Pantheon, 1980.
When Bad Things Happen to Good People, Harold Kushner. New York, N.Y.: Schocken Books, 1981.
When Living Hurts, Sol Gordon. New York, N.Y.: Union of American Hebrew Congregations, 1985.
When Memory Comes, Saul Friedlander. New York, N.Y.: Farrar, Strauss, and Giroux, 1979.
Why Me?, Rosemary Kushner. Philadelphia, Penn.: Saunders, 1981.

Aufbau, 2121 Broadway, New York, N.Y. 10023.
Medical Tribune, 257 Park Avenue, South, New York, N.Y. 10010.